The fisherman's guide to
Sea
Fishing

Marshall Cavendish London & New York

Published by Marshall Cavendish Books Limited
58 Old Compton Street
London W1V 5PA

©Marshall Cavendish Limited 1977, 1978, 1979

This material was first published by
Marshall Cavendish Limited in the
publication *Fisherman's Handbook*

First printed in 1979

Printed in Great Britain

ISBN 0 85685 695 9

Introduction

Unlike other branches of fishing, which have been in existence for several hundred years, sea fishing as a sport has developed only during the twentieth century. It is a direct descendent of the commercial method with handlines. Today, the techniques involved have become specialised into three main categories: harbour fishing, beachcasting and boat fishing.

The Fisherman's Guide to Sea Fishing approaches its subject under four main headings beginning with the most common species the angler is likely to encounter, depending upon the style of fishing that he prefers. Each species is dealt with from the point of view of habitat, life-cycle, food preferences and the baits which are likely to attract them. Fishing equipment is considered in the second section which covers all types of tackle requirements for boat and shore work. Bait has a section to itself and all the common baits are considered, together with information about collection and preparation. The book then enlarges upon the techniques involved in each branch of sea angling and includes a short chapter about weather—a necessary consideration for the sea fisherman whether he fishes from a boat anchored at an off-shore mark or casts from the shore of a rocky coastline. Finally, a small section is devoted to boats—both small boats for in-shore work and cruisers for use on the open sea.

The Fisherman's Guide to Sea Fishing caters to a wide range of fishing requirements. Whether he is a beginner or an enthusiast of long standing, every angler should find something of interest in these pages.

Contents

Sea
Fishing

Cod

The North Atlantic cod, *Gadus morhua,* is widespread off the coasts of Britain, especially Scotland, where it comes to feed from the deep water breeding grounds round Iceland. The cod, with herring and other 'round' fish, forms a major part of the huge commercial fisheries and vast quantities are trawled each year, the cod catch itself often exceeding 250,000 tons.

Colour variation

As with many species, the cod shows considerable colour variation dependent upon area, but it is usually a green/grey speckled with brown on the flanks and top, with a white belly. The lateral line is white and very distinct. There are three dorsal and two anal fins and these, coupled with the huge mouth of the cod, all contribute to making hard work for the angler who has to reel a big one up from perhaps 35 fathoms (210ft). The cod, like many members of its family—hake, whiting, pouting, coalfish, haddock, ling— has a long barbule on the lower jaw. During spawning a female cod

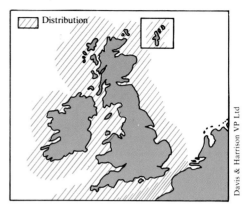

Davis & Harrison VP Ltd

Habitat

Cod inhabit deep water all round the British Isles for most of the year. At spawning time, which varies according to local conditions and the kind of year, they move to shallower water, to the coast. Most cod migrate south in winter, to return north in the spring.

Bait

Wherever cod fishing is done, the best baits are fish strip, shellfish, squid and lugworm.

Rod Sutterby,

Mike Prichard,

Cod

can release up to 9,000,000 eggs in midwater. This enormous number ensures that a sufficient percentage of tiny fish will evade the predations of other fish, birds, disease and natural disasters in order to ensure the continuity of the species.

The eggs hatch into $\frac{3}{16}$ larvae, growing to about an inch after three months. After early feeding on tiny marine organisms, the codling begin to eat fish, sandeels at first, then herring, haddock and other codling.

Fewer—but larger

It was commonplace ten years ago to take a boat not far out from Dover, Ramsgate, Deal, Hastings, and other South East Coast places, and bring in 50lb of prime cod and codling (all cod of up to 6lb are called codling). But the same does not apply today. Now fish are caught in fewer numbers throughout the year, but over a greater area, even off the West Coast, especially if one can fish deep. There, surprisingly, cod of 42lb and 43lb were taken a couple of years ago. Cod fishing seasons vary from one part of the British Isles to another. In the Clyde the big shoals arrive during February and March, where fish of 40lb have been caught in some numbers. Off the Isle of Mull in Scotland, June, July and August are the best fishing months. On the South and East Coasts, November, December and January are the traditional months to expect cod. Down in the West Country cod are caught throughout the year, not many, but a steady trickle of big fish that have become permanent residents in the areas of wrecks and pinnacles. Most of the Scottish venues have a resident population of small and medium-sized cod which live permanently on the inshore marks, but the larger fish are seasonal visitors which

The inexperienced angler may not be able to readily distinguish between the red cod, the codling and the pollack. Colour variation in the cod derives from local water conditions. They are both distinguishable from the pollack by a white lateral line and a receding lower lip with a barbule.

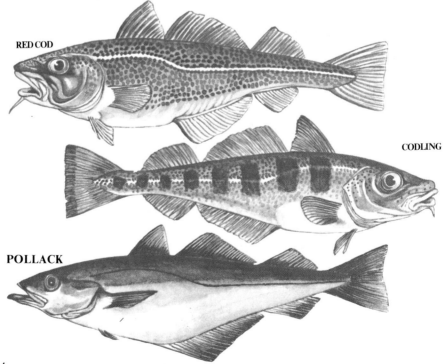

RED COD

CODLING

POLLACK

4

appear either to spawn or to take advantage of a natural glut of bait-fish or crustaceans.

All this is a pointer to the 'new-look' cod fishing that exists today. The East Coast and eastern end of the English Channel were once the big cod areas, with a long-beaten record cod of 32lb coming from Lowestoft. All this has changed, the angler seeking 32-pounders going South West or North East.

Close-in cod

It is not necessary to go boat-fishing in order to catch sizable cod. There are many beaches, such as Dungeness, in Kent, and many others round the coasts where cod can be caught on beachcasting tackle. Piers, groynes and moles, too, offer close-in

deepwater fishing for the species. Notable among these is the detached mole at Dover, where numbers of double-figure cod are taken every year when there is a run of the fish. Fishing stations such as these can be found in many areas. Yorkshire offers some wonderful cod fishing at places such as Filey Brigg and up to Flamborough Head.

The current record cod caught from a boat weighed 53lb and fell to G. Martin, fishing at Start Point, Devon, in 1972. There are now both boat and shore records, the latter of which is a 44lb 8oz cod caught in 1966 by B. Jones, from Toms Point, Barry, Glamorgan. While these sizes will be admired by anglers whose usual cod (when he can catch one) is in

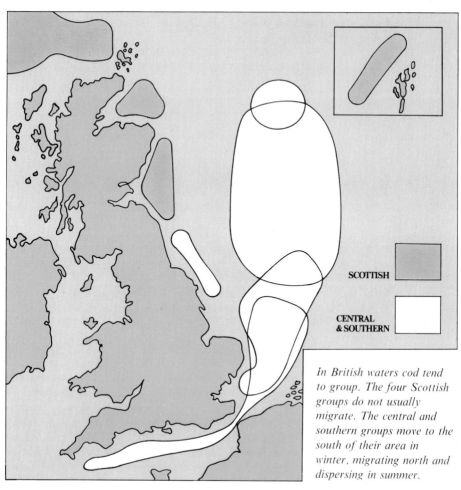

SCOTTISH

CENTRAL & SOUTHERN

In British waters cod tend to group. The four Scottish groups do not usually migrate. The central and southern groups move to the south of their area in winter, migrating north and dispersing in summer.

Cod

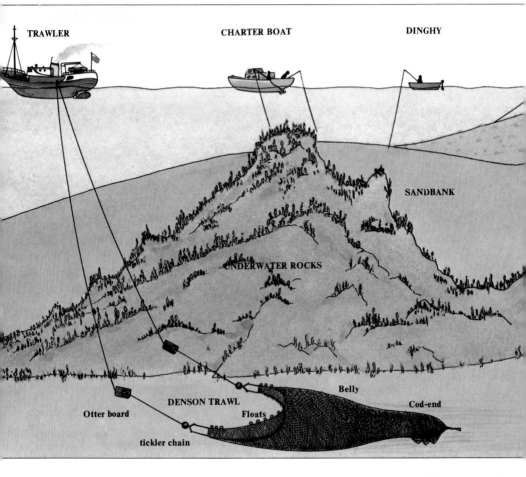

TRAWLER

CHARTER BOAT

DINGHY

SANDBANK

UNDERWATER ROCKS

Belly

DENSON TRAWL

Cod-end

Otter board

Floats

tickler chain

the 10lb region, the rod-caught records do not compare with commercially-trawled cod, some of which are known to weigh 200lb.

Feeding habits

The feeding habits of the cod are as wide as any fish. The gape of its mouth enables this fish to swallow vast amounts of edible—and inedible— matter, including white objects, which seem to attract it particularly. This habit has led to the development of white attractor spoons on cod tackle.

Many anglers over-estimate the strength of cod when choosing cod fishing tackle. This is particularly true of the average boat angler who tends to choose a really strong rod. But this is not necessary. After an initial

strong plunge or two it will come up if a steady line-retrieve is made; the large open mouth will provide most of the resistance. Despite their general greediness and large average size, cod can often be shy biters. Many an angler has struck at a tiny, twitchy bite only to find that he has connected solidly with a really big fish. On the South Coast where fierce Channel tides can make fishing difficult many cod anglers now use a wire line rather than a nylon monofilament line to get the bait down to where the fish are feeding.

Wire-line fishing

The wire has its own built-in weight and being far finer than nylon it creates less drag in the tide so that comparatively light leads can be used even in strong tidal runs. Wire-

SHORE ANGLER ROCK ANGLER

LEDGE

SEASHORE

SEABED

*Commercial fishing trawlers
will avoid the seashore,
sandbanks and underwater
rocks. These areas will then
be left to the angler on the
shore or in a boat.*

*Spots like Flamborough
Head in Yorkshire (above)
provide large winter catches
of cod. Beach fishing at
Folkestone in Kent (below)
a popular cod venue.*

line fishing for cod has become something of a science and various kinds of line have been marketed in an attempt to cut down the weight, size, and thus the diameter even further. Many anglers believe wire lines to be dangerous. But they only become dangerous when they get snagged up on the sea bed and someone tries to free them by heaving on the line with his bare hands, when the wire can cut like a razor. If stout gloves are used the danger is eliminated entirely. Wire is almost essential in very deep water, where its weight takes the bait down without the necessity of using big 2lb leads.

Techniques

The techniques for catching cod include all the standard methods: ledgering with fish strips, lugworm, squid; paternostering with soft crab, whole small pouting, and so on; pirks and lures, and feathering. Cod, too, can be taken from deep water, from close offshore marks, from piers, rocks and beaches, and from the tops of 100ft-high Yorkshire cliffs! Here the safety factor is a vital element in strong winter winds.

Eric Birch

The cod's huge mouth (above) allows it to scoop up many foods, including fish, crustaceans, weeds, and even tin cans and disposable cups (above right) from the sea bed. A rig incorporating a section of a plastic cup (below right) has been used with some success by cod fishermen.

Rod Sutterby

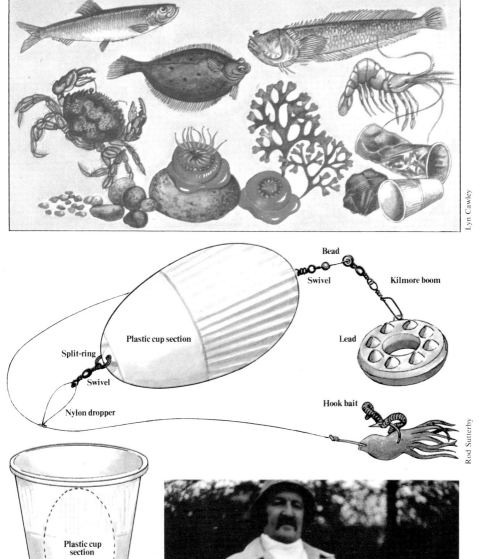

Lyn Cawley

Rod Sutterby

A 35lb cod taken while boat fishing in winter several miles out from Newhaven on the Sussex coast. This fish was caught on the bottom with squid.

Bill Howes

9

Pollack

The author has two favourite fish: the porbeagle shark, for its tremendous endurance when fighting at the end of a line, and the pollack (*Pollachius pollachius*) because it is a fish that, when hooked, has an exhilarating first run. With the pollack, words such as 'power dive' seem accurate. This member of the cod family can be one of our sporting fishes provided it is taken over a suitable habitat and on tackle that responds to the fish's struggles.

To get the best from most sea fish, they have to be fought in shallow water. This is particularly true of the pollack, a fish of reefs and rocky bottoms, living and feeding among the tangles of kelp. The pollack comes inshore in the spring, just as the sun begins to bring warmth and fertility to the littoral waters. It is a predatory species that feeds higher in the water than the other cod-like fish. Of course, the pollack will also feed on crustaceans and molluscs but the species is particularly adapted to hunting other fish.

The pollack is sleek, well-proportioned, immensely powerful, and built for ambushing other reef-dwelling species. It tends to shoal up according to size. Most of the inshore rock areas will have a population of smallish pollack which feed on the fry of other fish that spawn in the shallows. As summer progresses, the larger pollack come in from deeper water, feeding over the top of the reef, particularly in the late evening and into the hours of darkness. During the day, especially in strong sunlight, these larger fish sink down to the sides of pinnacle rocks, among the weeds and broken ground.

Confusion between pollack and coalfish

There is always some confusion, among novice anglers, between the pollack and its near relative, the coalfish, despite quite clear identification points. The pollack is green-brown with a dark lateral line that curves sharply over the pectoral before straightening as it continues back along the body to the squared-off tail. Among juvenile fish there can be a colour variation that is environmental. A highly coloured habitat,

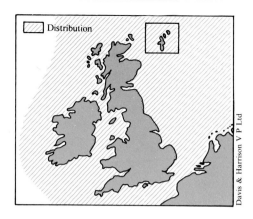

Davis & Harrison V P Ltd

Rod Sutterby

Habitat

The pollack lives over rock pinnacles and above the wrecks off the South West coast. This species also exists in brackish esturial waters and rocky areas such as Trevose Head, North Cornwall (below)

Baits

Mackerel strip, imitating small fish, is the favoured bait, but the pollack can also be taken on spoons.

Mike Millman

Pollack

with a mass of red weed, for example, will influence the basic hue of the fish.

The pollack has a protruding lower jaw, an unmistakable recognition feature, indicating that it feeds by attacking its prey from below. There are three dorsal fins, as in most of the cod family, and the body is less rounded than that of the coalfish.

The coalfish *(Pollachius virens)* is thicker-bodied and is blue-black when adult but olive green before maturity. The lateral line is white and straight. The jaws are similar in length, although in the larger, deep-water specimens there is evidence of an elongated underjaw, similar to that of mature pollack. Coalfish have a barbule under the lower jaw, but you will have to search hard for this rudimentary protuberance. Another major feature which distinguishes the species is that the tail in the coalfish is clearly forked.

Both species are found over rocky ground and offshore wrecks. The coalfish seems to be more northerly in its distribution, with a lot of small fish permanently in residence on the Eastern coastline. Pollack are a South-Western species fond of the rocky coasts of the British mainland and the Atlantic shores of Ireland. Both fish come into shallow areas, but the coalfish tends to seek a slightly deeper habitat. Pollack are found in some estuaries – they can tolerate an amount of freshwater – whereas the coalfish is rarely found in a brackish environment.

Spawning period

Both fish spawn early in the year. Pollack spawn between February and May, depending on geographical location. Fish living in southern waters spawn earlier than those from a more northerly habitat. They seek deep water – of 50 fathoms or more – in early autumn, at which time the species figures importantly in trawler catches. The 'coalie' generally spawns in much deeper water in March, when as many as four million eggs are released by the larger females. The eggs are pelagic, floating and drifting on the ocean currents. They hatch into larvae about $\frac{1}{8}$th of an inch in length. These larval pollack

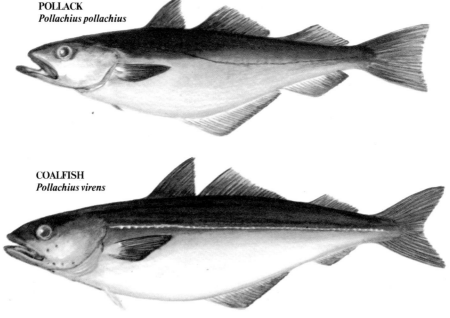

POLLACK
Pollachius pollachius

COALFISH
Pollachius virens

Ralph Stobart

Mike Millman

(Above) The coalfish and two of the characteristics that differentiate this species from the pollack. Note the white lateral line and paired jaws.

(Right) Note how the pollack's lower jaw is protruding, an aid to a predatory fish that attacks from below. This species does not have a chin barbule.

(Left) How to recognize pollack and coalfish.

John Holden

and coalfish form shoals and feed on drifting animals in the plankton stream. The tidal drift and onshore winds will move the shoals of fry into shallow coastal water, where they remain for their first year of life, feeding on copepods among the kelp and weed fronds. Both pollack and coalfish fry grow quickly and when about an inch long move out into reef areas, where the feeding is better in quality and quantity.

With the advent of West Country wreck fishing, things really began to happen, records being set and broken almost every week. The wrecks provided an untapped source of fish for the deep-anchoring techniques developed by anglers in ports like Brixham and Plymouth. The original in-

tention was to get baits down to the massive conger that fill the wrecks. Inevitably, some anglers concentrated on the layer of water over the bulk of the wreck. Giant cod, ling, pollack, coalfish, pouting and sea bream began to figure among the catches, the artificial lure making its mark as the principal method for this form of fishing.

Two basic styles

Pollack fishing divides neatly into two basic styles – letting a bait or lure down to fish, and working a moving lure across a habitat, either by spinning or trolling from a boat. In the first case, the angler is normally concerned with large fish, either from a wreck or reef. As there are a number of species that can be expected to come to the bait, the

13

Pollack

tackle is often too heavy for pollack. A technique based on a sink-and-draw working of the bait in mid-water does allow a degree of selection. To get the best sport from pollack, one must give them the opportunity to develop the powerful runs of which they are so capable.

Terminal tackle

In terms of terminal tackle and rigs, there is little to separate reef and wreck fishing. Simplicity, and a trace that gives life to the bait, are very important. You can fish a single hook to ledger rig, but I prefer a simple paternostered bait, using the weight on a 'rotten bottom' line of weak nylon that if snagged on rocks or tangled among the standing rigging of a wreck, can by broken out without losing what could be a good fish.

The trace must be long enough to give the bait an opportunity to swim naturally with the tide. Pollack will be chasing smaller fish, so anything that has an attractive, lifelike appearance will be taken. Use a 3ft trace when the tide is slack, extending this to 6ft or more when it begins to run hard.

Obviously, some consideration must be given to the length of trace that can be handled from whatever boat you are fishing from. The author incorporates a fixed boom, of twisted stainless steel wire or swivelled brass, into the rig. Its purpose is to keep the hook trace standing off the reel line when the gear is being lowered, for all too often a simple nylon paternoster will tangle the bait around the reel line if lowered too fast. A weak nylon sinker link of about 3ft is ideal. The rig is lowered to the reef or wreck and stopped immediately any solid ground or obstruction is felt, and the line is wound back a couple of turns. This will allow the bait to swim freely just above the habitat. Sooner or later, the weight will be held fast, but breaking out will only lose the lead.

The presentation of the bait is critical. A great lump of mackerel or herring can never be as attractive as a properly cut and mounted bait. I slice off a diagonal lask of fish bait about 6in long and tie it to the hook with elasticated thread. Presented like this,

(Above) Feathers used for jigging lures for pollack, coalfish and ling.

Stainless Steel Wire Boom

Monofilament Trace
For Slack Tide 3ft
For Running Tide 6ft

DEEP WATER

WRASSE

RAGWO

CRAB

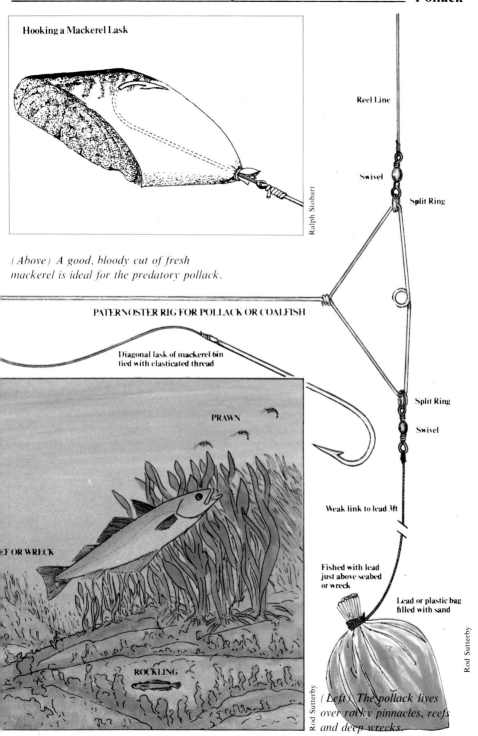

Hooking a Mackerel Lask

Ralph Stobart

(*Above*) *A good, bloody cut of fresh mackerel is ideal for the predatory pollack.*

Reel Line

Swivel

Split Ring

PATERNOSTER RIG FOR POLLACK OR COALFISH

Diagonal lask of mackerel 6in tied with elasticated thread

Split Ring

Swivel

Weak link to lead 3ft

Fished with lead just above seabed or wreck

Lead or plastic bag filled with sand

PRAWN

F OR WRECK

ROCKLING

Rod Sutterby

Rod Sutterby

(*Left*) *The pollack lives over rocky pinnacles, reefs and deep wrecks.*

15

(Above) Land's End, a fine pollack mark.
(Left) Pollack caught on a red/silver pirk.

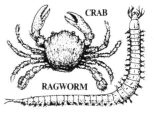

CRAB

RAGWORM

Mike Millman

the bait is not easily torn from the hook.

Pollack take a bait in a great many different ways but, once in their mouths, it will be carried back to the fish's lie. That is when the angler gets the thrill of pollack fishing. As the fish feels pressure on the line it will nose-dive back to the reef. Let it go, having previously set a reasonable playing drag to the reel. Try to turn the fish so that it does not take the rig into an obstruction.

Pinnacle rock fishing is top of the league for the pollack fisherman. Here, the prey can be smallish shoal fish swimming in groups over the tips of the pinnacles, or the solitary big specimen that hugs the sheer rock faces or loiters in the crevices. The angling style

depends on the depth of water over the peaks. The deepwater reef can be fished with natural bait or pirks; the relatively shallow water reef can be trolled, or worked progressively with a lure, from a drifting boat.

Artificial lures for pollack

There are two successful kinds of artificial lure for pollack fishing – I hesitate to call them spinners because not all lures actually spin – the large metal spoon that wobbles and flashes as it curves through the water, and the bar spoon, of which the German Sprat is probably the best-known pattern. Spoons are easy to fish, whether they are being cast or trolled behind a boat, because they have weight and are, in the main,

(Right) Plump 25lb 10oz Mevagissey coalfish.
(Below) Natural foods of the pollack.

PRAWN

HERRING

ROCKLING

WRASSE

BLENNY

designed to work without additional weight.

Unfortunately, long-distance casting demands the addition of more weight to get the spoon out to the fish, while trolling at high speed requires more weight to sink the spoon. The problem with adding either a spiral or a Wye lead to the trace, ahead of the lure, is that the extra weight dampens the action of the artificial lure. It is, therefore, best to try to avoid using additional weights, and instead to choose a heavier lure. The traditional rubber eel, made from a piece of flexible gas tubing, was one of the finest lures ever. It has now been superseded by a number of man-made fish-shaped lures with action built in. Most of them work well, but

it is worrying that when reef fishing one expects to lose gear—most of it expensive.

Colour plays an important part in pollack fishing. As an attacker from below, one would expect the pollack to be responsive to silhouette and action. There is no doubt that these two factors are of prime importance, but there are times when pollack will take only a red eel, or a white, or, perhaps, a grubby white one. Has this something to do with the amount of light penetrating the water, and possibly, the prey that the fish expect to find at that time? Experiment even by using feathered lures, to represent fry.

Avoid heavy tackle, for pollack provide superb sport on balanced, light equipment.

17

Wrasse

BALLAN WRASSE
Labrus bergylta

Wrasse are beautiful fish. In the British Isles they are found in most coastal areas, where rock, weeds, molluscs and a few fathoms of sheltered inshore water provide a habitat.

The largest and most common wrasse is the ballan. It looks something like a freshwater carp, having one long dorsal fin set above a thick, muscled body. The fin has 19 or 20 spiny rays at the head end and 9–11 flexible rays towards the tail. The jaws are powerful, with lips designed for tearing limpets and other shellfish from rock faces. The teeth on the jaws are strong but there are no teeth on the palate. Instead the wrasse has pharyngeal teeth for grinding.

Ballan wrasse
Ballan wrasse occur in many colours, related to those predominating in their environment. Newcomers to shore fishing often make the mistake of identifying a number of different 'ballan' species because the fish vary so much. Generally, they are a greenish brown, often with a reddish belly dotted with white spots. The pectoral and pelvic fins are frequently red and spotted.

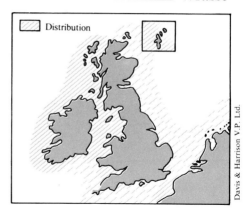

Distribution

Davis & Harrison V.P. Ltd.

Habitat

The colourful, fighting wrasse can be found wherever there are rocks and reefs holding the crustaceans and shellfish which the species feeds upon. Typical of wrasse ground is the shredded coast of Ireland's beautiful Dingle peninsula (below).

Baits

Rod Sutterby

Use small worm, shellfish or crustacean baits.

Mike Pritchard

The species favours a habitat where there is at least three or four fathoms of water at low water spring tides—probably because strong, lengthy kelps need a reasonable depth of water to grow in. These weeds provide ideal cover both for the wrasse and for the smaller creatures, such as crabs, lobsters, other crustaceans, and molluscs, on which the species feeds. Furthermore, during storms, areas of shallow water are much disturbed by strong surface movement, which drives these animals out from the security of the weeds into deeper, clean ground areas where they can be more easily caught by the predatory wrasse.

Smaller ballan tend to remain very close inshore for most of the year. Larger fish keep to deeper water, either below cliffs, where the water is often ten or more fathoms deep, or farther out to sea on offshore reefs rising clear of the seabed. In reefs, the fish live in the higher areas at depths of about ten fathoms. They are seldom found in shallow inshore areas as they need more food than such areas can generally provide.

(Above) The mouth of the wrasse, showing the strong jaw teeth present in these fishes. There are also teeth in the throat.
(Right) Rocky, weedy habitat of the wrasses.
(Below) Shellfish and crustaceans that form the food of the wrasse family.

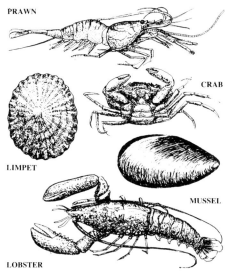

PRAWN

CRAB

LIMPET

MUSSEL

LOBSTER

20

Ballan wrasse do not form shoals, although there may well be an enormous population on a single reef. They have definite territorial behaviour, each patrolling a small area. This may be related to their breeding habits, for wrasse are one of the few fish to build nests. They spawn in late May–July in shallow water, making the nest from pieces of seaweed and debris which they jam into crevices between rocks. The eggs are then dispersed throughout the strands of weed that comprise the nest.

Slow growth of ballan wrasse

Ballan wrasse eggs are quite large, about a millimetre in diameter, with a distinct yellow colour. The fry measure about 2in in the first winter of life. With average feeding, they grow to 7in in two years.

Occasionally, the angler will hook a brightly coloured, smaller wrasse when fishing from the rocks. This may be any one of a number of lesser wrasse species, but the commonest is the cuckoo wrasse, *Labrus mixtus (L bimaculatus)*. This fish is more likely to be hooked in deeper water than the ballan, but does occasionally come near the cliffs. As with the ballan, beginners often wrongly identify more than one species of cuckoo. This is because the sexes are completely different in colour. Males are a striking blue with an orange-red hue to the top of the head and shoulders. Females are orange-red, with three dark spots under the end of the dorsal fin.

The cuckoo wrasse rarely exceeds 14in in length, with males always slightly larger than females of the same age. Both sexes are poor fighters, but add colour to any catch.

Another small wrasse (up to 9in), the corkwing, *Crenilabrus melops*, also varies greatly in colour, although the variation is not related to sex. One identification feature that is fairly reliable is the single dark spot in the centre of the tail wrist. In addition, the

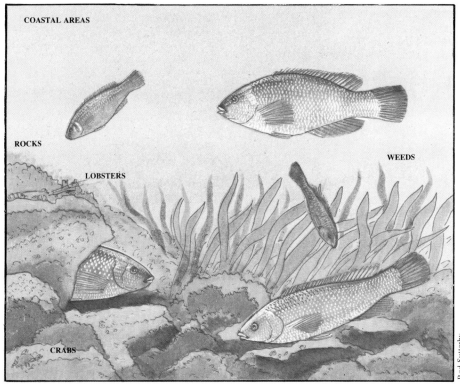

COASTAL AREAS

ROCKS

LOBSTERS

WEEDS

CRABS

Rod Sutterby

cheeks and underside of the jaws are streaked with lines of bright blue or green. The females have a protuberance just behind the vent. This is part of the egg-laying mechanism, although little is known of its precise function.

Corkwing and Goldsinny

The corkwing can be easily confused with another little wrasse, the goldsinny, *Ctenolabrus rupestris*, as both the size and shape of the two fish are similar. But whereas the corkwing is fairly brightly coloured, the goldsinny is a drab overall brownish-yellow. Nevertheless, it too has a single spot on the tail area, although this is on the upper rather than the central part of the wrist.

The goldsinny is fond of much deeper water than most wrasses, preferring depths of around 30 fathoms. It is small, averaging only 6in long, and is common only in the west of the British Isles.

Another small wrasse occasionally caught around Britain is the small-mouthed wrasse, or rock cook, *Centrolabrus exoletus*. Apart from its extremely small mouth, identifying features are its dorsal fin in which the soft rear part is slightly raised above the hard-rayed forepart, and the five spines at the leading end of its anal fin—all other wrasse have three. It also has a more northerly distribution than most other wrasse, being found in the North Atlantic and in the Baltic.

The last British wrasse is the rainbow, *Coris julis*. This is a brilliantly coloured and is common in the Bay of Biscay and down ·towards the tropics, but it is only a rare migrant to Britain and then only to south-western shores.

The rainbow wrasse is small—about 6in long—and has no scales on the head. It is alone among wrasse species in having elongated and pointed pectoral fins. The dorsal fin is set low on the body, with a raised and pointed leading edge to the hard-rayed

(*Above*) *The ballan wrasse is beautifully marked, as are all the members of the group. It is the largest British wrasse species, with a rod-caught shore record weight of 8lb 6oz 6dr, taken in 1976 from a beach in the Channel Isles.*
(*Left*) *Hooking a whole crab and lugworm, both tempting baits for the larger wrasses such as the ballan.*
(*Right*) *The kelp-strewn gullies of South Cornwall hold large numbers of the colourful wrasses.*

Ralph Stobart

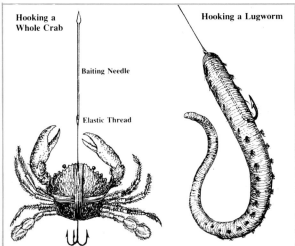

Hooking a Whole Crab

Hooking a Lugworm

Baiting Needle

Elastic Thread

section. Colour varies, although the predominant hue on male fish is purple, to which is added bright silver blotches and a lateral silver band. Females are less bright but have the same basic coloration.

The only wrasse of interest to anglers is the ballan. They are not large fish—adults reach about 20in—but they can be powerful fighters on light tackle. The fight, like the fish's colour, is largely conditioned by its environment. Strong tides, currents that sweep around rocky headlands, and crashing wave patterns that surge into gullies and

Mike Millman

channels, all add power to the run of a hooked ballan.

Light tackle is also important in protecting the fish from hurried pressure changes. The swimbladder is not connected to the gullet, so that the fish cannot quickly equalize pressure as it is winched to the surface. This unfortunately means that a lot of splendid fish are released only to die.

Wrasse 'just give up'

A protracted fight can also bring about the death of a wrasse. It seems that they sometimes just give up life after being brought ashore. No amount of gentleness when unhooking them revives the will to live.

Wrasse can be caught throughout the year, although fishing is best between May and November, as in the winter fish move into deeper, warmer water. Nor is there any particular time of day to fish, for they can be caught throughout the entire period of daylight. This makes the species popular with anglers, for the hottest of summer days and slackest tide will produce wrasse.

Two times when wrasse do cease to cooperate, however, are at night and during hard weather, when breakers surge far up the cliff faces. Wrasse disappear into a safe hole in bad weather. Likewise, the sensible angler stays away from cliffs and ledges that are a hazard when the wind howls.

Mike Millman

Plaice

Of all the fishes caught around the British Isles, few are better known than the plaice (*Pleuronectes platessa*). It has long been a favourite with the housewife as it looks very attractive when displayed on fishmongers' slabs with its eye-catching orange/red spots. The plaice belongs to the order of fish known as Heterosomata, which means 'twisted-bodied'. These are the flatfishes which swim on one or other side of their body just above the sea bottom.

The plaice lies and swims left side down. The colouring of its right or upper side varies from a light sandy brown right through to a dark brown according to the locality and the type of seabed on which it lives. The distinctive spots, too, range in colour from pale orange to bright scarlet. Furthermore, if the seabed is chalky, then it is not uncommon to catch plaice with white spots as well as red. The underside, however, is always a translucent bluish white with thin blue streaks.

The skin of the plaice feels completely smooth when rubbed with the finger, although there are several bony knobs on the ridge of the head which distinguish it from other flatfish. The lateral line is very slightly curved in the vicinity of the pectoral fin, and the jaws are lined with very strong teeth. There are also muscles resembling a second set of jaws at the entrance of the gullet, which are used to crush small shellfish.

Plaice distribution

Plaice are found all around the British Isles, extending northwards as far as Iceland and as far south as the Mediterranean. Spawning takes place very early in the year— usually in January or February—in depths of 15-30 fathoms. The eggs float in the sea and measure approximately $\frac{1}{10}$in in diameter. A good-sized female, a fish of, say, around 3lb, produces as many as 250,000 eggs in one spawning. Depending on the water temperature, the eggs take anything from 8-28 days to hatch. The newly hatched larvae measure about $\frac{1}{3}$in, and at this stage are not flat but rounded like other fish.

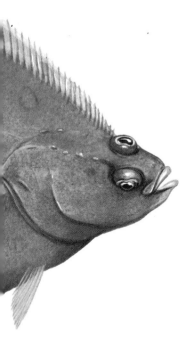

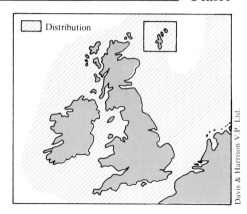

Rod Sutterby

Habitat

The plaice, Pleuronectes platessa, *held in high esteem as a table fish, prefers to live in sandy areas such as Morte Bay, seen below looking south-west from the rocks at Mortenhoe. It is common all round the coast of the British Isles.*

Baits

Although bivalve eaters, plaice are usually caught on lug or ragworm.

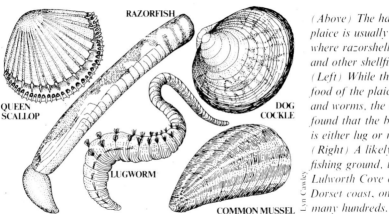

RAZORFISH

QUEEN SCALLOP

DOG COCKLE

LUGWORM

COMMON MUSSEL

(Above) The habitat of the plaice is usually an area where razorshell, mussels and other shellfish live. (Left) While the natural food of the plaice is bivalves and worms, the angler has found that the best hookbait is either lug or ragworm. (Right) A likely plaice fishing ground, the beautiful Lulworth Cove on the Dorset coast, only one of many hundreds.

The larva feeds on its yolk sac for about the first week of its existence and normally not until it has exhausted this food supply does it change from its original round shape to the flat shape it will have for the rest of its life. At the same time, the young plaice begins to take in food, which at first is, of course, of microscopic dimensions.

The fish's change in shape begins with a change in the position of the eyes. The left eye moves upwards and forwards and after about ten days arrives on the upper margin of the head just in front of the right eye. A little over four weeks later it reaches its final position above and in front of the right eye. While the eyes are going through this rotating movement, the young fish begins to take up a new position when swimming. As it has been growing, the whole anatomy of the body has gradually undergone a distinct twisting process, and the fully developed fish finally swims on its left side with both eyes pointing upwards.

Plaice growth rate

The growth rate of a plaice, though relatively fast for a flatfish, is slow when compared with that of cod, for instance. A four-year-old fish will measure only 12-13in, although this may vary slightly from area to area. Females mature some time between their third and seventh years, when they are about 9-11in long. Males mature a year earlier, between their second and sixth years.

The early life of a plaice is spent in sandy

shallows feeding on very small crustaceans called copepods and large quantities of mollusc larvae. After about six months of this diet the fish attain a length of about 2in, and at about this size they gradually move farther out from the shore, although they still favour areas where the depth is less than five fathoms. Tagging experiments have shown that plaice do not as a rule travel a very great distance, usually staying close to the area where they were spawned throughout their life. There is one fish on record that was tagged in the North Sea in 1904. It was recaptured in 1920 only a few miles from where it had originally been tagged.

After spawning

Adult plaice return to shallower waters near the shore in March and April to recover from the rigours of spawning. At this time they are thin, but after a few weeks of feeding in the rich shallows they quickly regain weight. The adult fish feed mainly on bivalve shellfish of all kinds, small cockles and mussels being firm favourites. The mussels are swallowed whole and are crushed by the jaw-like muscles in the throat; the fish then digests the contents and excretes the shell.

If there is ample food, plaice will frequent almost any type of seabed. Some of the best catches are taken in very rocky areas where they are usually feeding on mussels growing on the sides of the rocks. On sandy seabeds they search out razorfish and they will even travel up estuaries in search of cockles and other bivalves. Occasionally, too, they will eat marine worms, such as lugworms and ragworms, although these do not seem to figure very prominently in the plaice's natural diet. Therefore, it is not surprising that, although trawlers catch great quantities of plaice, rod and line anglers fishing the same area with marine worms usually fail to make big catches.

The most likely area to take plaice on rod and line is on mussel beds—but the mussels should be smallish, no bigger than an inch in length. Mussel beds appear in different areas from year to year, and they are usually

Robin Fletcher

27

Plaice

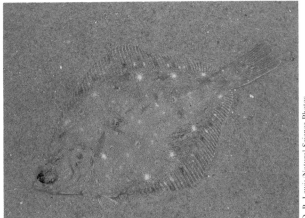

(Left) A fine example of camouflage: a plaice at rest on sand. The fish's pigment cells respond to the colour and pattern of the fish's background and imitate it to an amazing degree. (Right) A still-fresh 6lb 8oz plaice caught by well-known angler Bill Herme. (Below) A paternoster trace with a plastic attractor, and the same attractor used with a running ledger.

D. B. Lewis/Natural Science Photos

located by accident, but once found it is reasonably safe to assume there are plaice to be caught there in good numbers.

The ideal time to try for these 'flatties' is during prolonged settled weather during the summer. Clear water and bright sun make for better fishing. As the fish feed largely on bivalves, one would assume that these would be the best bait, but for some reason they seem reluctant to take them when they have been removed from their shells; and of course it is totally impracticable to try to hook the mussel while still inside its shell. Thus the angler is reduced to using less favoured, but nevertheless successful, marine worms as bait. Lugworm usually proves the best, with ragworm running a close second, although this order may be reversed in some areas. Peeler crab, too, is often used.

Size potential

Plaice do not grow to great size and the rod-caught record is a fish of 10lb $3\frac{1}{2}$oz, boated by H Gardiner fishing in Longa Sound, Scotland in 1974. Professional trawlers frequently take bigger fish than this, often well into double figures, but the rod and line angler can usually count himself lucky if he takes fish in the 3–4lb range. For this reason a light hollow glass rod in the 20lb class is to be recommended, providing leads of over 12oz are not going to be used.

For terminal tackle a trace should be used when the tide is running, but paternoster

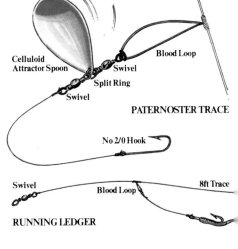

Celluloid Attractor Spoon **Blood Loop** **Swivel** **Split Ring** **Swivel**

PATERNOSTER TRACE

No 2/0 Hook

Swivel **Blood Loop** **8ft Trace**

RUNNING LEDGER

gear is favoured on sluggish tides or slack water. If using a trace, it should be about 8ft in length, either fished through a Clements boom or a Kilmore boom. If baiting with lugworm, a long-shanked hook, No. 2 or 1, is quite large enough. Use three hooks together, as more than one fish is taken at a time quite regularly. This is often because, even if you are holding the rod when the plaice swallows the worm, no bite is detected due to their having the nasty habit of swallowing the baited hook and remaining still. It is only when you lift the rod tip that you realize that a fish has taken the bait.

Fish caught like this are usually deeply hooked. If, however, a bite is felt it is usually

Mike Millman

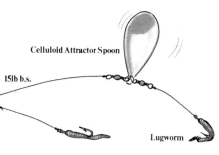

Celluloid Attractor Spoon

15lb b.s.

Lugworm

Rod Sutterby

second, every time the lead strikes the seabed it sends up a cloud of 'dust' which, because plaice are very curious creatures, brings them close to the baited hooks to investigate. Fishing this way, the bite is very positive, being more in the nature of a sudden snatch rather than the gentle tap experienced with a trace. Unlike a bite on a trace, the sudden snatch should be struck immediately. Once hooked, the fish dives for the seabed and on light gear can put up quite a lively fight, diving for the bottom all the way to the boat. A landing net should be used in preference to a gaff for the bigger specimens.

Although plaice generally favour deeper water than other flatfish such as dabs and flounders, good fish can also be taken by shore-based anglers. However, whereas boat anglers will go out and fish specifically for plaice, plaice taken by shore anglers are more often caught by accident than design. Most likely areas for shore plaice are river mouths, particularly those of Devon and Cornwall. Notable fish can be caught from the shore, too. A former record fish was landed by a youngster fishing at Salcombe, Devon.

Estuaries and bays

When fishing for plaice in estuaries, the baited spoon method is the best. By slowly recovering line the bait is kept on the move, so preventing attack by the crabs which abound in this kind of area. In addition, the spoon as it revolves flashes and disturbs the seabed, attracting fish to the area. As well as estuaries, other likely shore-based spots are sheltered sandy bays with a fair depth of water, and rocky shores with sandy gullies. For the latter, a paternoster rig is recommended, the terrain being too rock-covered and snaggy to use a spoon.

Plaice make excellent eating. A fish of over $2\frac{1}{2}$lb can be 'quarter filleted'. To do this, cut through to the bone from head to tail along the lateral line with a sharp knife and then carefully remove the flesh from the bone by cutting outwards towards the fins. Do this on both the top and the underside, thus making four good fillets. A fish in good condition will produce half its total weight in fillets.

only a light tap, tap, and should be left for the fish to gorge the bait. To avoid the temptation of striking too soon, it is best not even to hold the rod.

To attract the fish, white spoons may be added to the trace, but they must be celluloid and not metal. Celluloid spoons are lighter and even a slight tide will give them movement in the water, and it is this movement that attracts flatfish to the hooks.

Slack-water fishing

A different method of fishing should be used when using paternoster gear on slack water. In these conditions, the rod tip should be continually raised and lowered. This has two effects: first, it gives the bait movement;

Sharks

SIX-GILLED SHARK
Hexanchus griseus

Twenty-five or so species of fish belonging to the shark order have been recorded in the waters around the British Isles. One of these species, the basking shark, *Cetorhinus maximus,* although relatively common, cannot be considered as a potential angling species as it is a plankton feeder unwilling to take any bait presented by an angler.

Nine other species are nearly always found in water well beyond that fished by anglers. Since these species are bottom-dwellers which swim at the edge of the continental shelf, they too can be removed from the list of species taken by anglers. Eight species are taken with great regularity on many parts of the coast but are not considered as sharks because of their small size, or names. These are the tope and smoothhound, the spotted dogfish—lesser, greater (bull huss), blackmouthed—the spurdog, and monkfish which is also a true shark.

The remaining species are all large members of the family which are considered by anglers as real sharks. At least two of these,

the blue shark, *Prionace glauca,* and the porbeagle, *Lamna nasus,* are extremely common at certain times of the year in some places, while two other species, the mako, *Isurus oxyrinchus,* and the thresher shark *Alopias vulpinus,* make the angling press with some regularity. A recent addition to the list of rod-and-line captured species is the six-gilled shark, *Hexanchus griseus.* There is only one recorded in Britain so far.

Several other species are known to frequent our waters. Reports exist for the bramble shark, *Echinorhinus brucus,* Greenland shark, *Somniosus microcephalus* and, surprisingly, the hammerhead, *Sphyrna sp.,* which has been claimed (unsubstantiated) as a rod and line capture. Reported sightings only, without the evidence of an actual specimen, are the rigger shark, *Galeocerdo cuvier,* and white shark, *Carcharodon carchararias.*

The capture by rod and line of any of the last five, even six, species must be considered as luck rather than reward for intentional

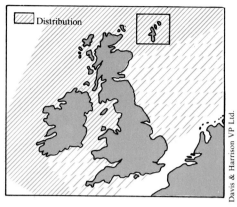

Davis & Harrison VP Ltd.

Habitat

Sharks are mainly roving fishes, seeking their food in the expanse of deep waters. Where food fishes congregate off cliffs and rocks, sharks will often come close to the shore at places such as the Hoy area off Orkney (below).

Baits

Whole dead fish of many kinds, especially the oily ones, are excellent shark baits.

Rod Sutterby

Mike Millman

31

angling effort and any angler trying specifically for these would spend many fruitless days before reward came his way, if at all.

Nevertheless since fortune does smile on some anglers, no description of the sharks found around Britain can be complete without them. Since all sharks conform more than most fish to a general shape or body form which consists essentially of a conical head with mouth on the underside and long tapering cylindrical body which ends in a forked tail, only those features which differentiate them need be discussed.

The hammerhead

The hammerhead is immediately recognizable because the head is flattened from above and below and extended laterally into an unmistakable shape. The reason for this strange modification is not understood. There have been many suggestions about functional adaptation. One is that the wide placing of the olefactory organs at the extremities of the 'hammer' may have given the shark a 'stereoscopic' sense of smell.

Another species, the thresher, also immediately identifies itself because of the extended length of the upper half of the tail of the fish. Again, proof of function for such a long tail is lacking. It has been suggested that the tail is used first to herd food fish into

HAMMERHEAD SHARK
Sphyrna zygaena

a tight pack and then for stunning them.

Some other shark species can also be easily identified because they deviate from a general pattern shown by most sharks. Assuming that all sharks have two dorsal fins, a large one followed by a second smaller one near the tail, any shark not showing the two fins, but only a single large one near the tail, should also possess six gill openings on each side of the head and not five. This identifies the six-gilled shark.

In a somewhat similar way, the absence of an anal fin (the fin situated between the pelvic fins and the tail) means that the specimen in question is a member of the

Shark can be identified by their teeth. These jaws show those of the mako.

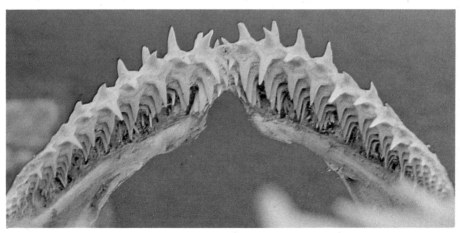

Rod Sutterby

(Above) One of the rarer sharks, the hammerhead. (Below) An Irish blue caught off Baltimore.

spurdog family, for all sharks which have cylindrical bodies but lack an anal fin belong to this group whether they bear spines at the front edge of the two dorsal fins or not. Such a shark would be either a bramble or a Greenland shark. Distinction between these two species is very easy, for while the skin of the Greenland shark is rough like all sharks, the bramble shark also has many large thorns similar to those on the roker or thornback ray. The English name, bramble, is therefore, very apt.

The other sharks, the porbeagle, mako, blue, tiger and white do not show any of the features mentioned above, i.e. the absence of or special development of any fins, but conform completely to the generalized picture of a fish with five pairs of gill openings, two dorsal fins and an anal fin. But body proportions, fin positions, colour and shape of teeth, are aids to identification.

Blue and tiger sharks

The blue shark has an extremely long, slim body with the upper part of the tail much larger than its lower part, narrow, long pectoral fins and vivid blue colour. A shark with a blunt, short snout and short pectorals, highly asymmetrical tail, and grey or transverse bars would be a tiger shark.

Three species remain, the porbeagle, mako and white shark. They bear the greatest

Bill Howes

resemblance to one another and are closely related. Indeed the similarity between the porbeagle and mako is so great that it was once not realised that the mako existed in British waters. A world record claim to the International Game Fishing Association (IGFA) for a record porbeagle showed that mako exist in our seas, for on examination the fish was identified as a mako, not a porbeagle, on the basis of tooth structure.

Had the captor known that the mako is characterized by very long, slim triangular teeth, unlike the triangular teeth of the porbeagle where the main triangle is flanked by one very small triangular cusp at the base, the mistake would not have been made. Again, the porbeagle tends to be much more squat or plump than the mako, and always shows two caudal keels, one large, the other much smaller and less distinct. The mako only has one keel, due to the flattening of the body just in front of the tail.

Any shark taken off Britain which externally resembles the porbeagle but has only one caudal keel should also be examined for tooth shape. If they are triangular, with serrated edges then—at long last—a British white shark will have been taken.

The blue shark is a southern species which prefers warm water. As an oceanic fish it arrives off Britain's South Coast and south and west coasts of Ireland with the coming of summer, but keeps well off shore. Its main distribution area is off Cornwall both on the English Channel side and to the north and it is only at the end of exceptionally warm summers that some may move north into the Irish Sea. Off Ireland many are found off the south and south-west and along certain areas in the west such as Galway Bay.

Floats for sharking are not the subtle things the freshwater angler uses. This is a novel screw clamp stopper.

Some may move north to appear in the autumn off the west coast of Scotland, but because the waters of the Minch (between the mainland and the Outer Hebrides) have only a northern and southern access to the open sea, few blue shark are found in that area. Most records from these northern waters come from west of the Hebrides, from the Rockall and St Kilda area.

A similar distribution exists for the mako shark. However, the numbers caught each year are nowhere near as great as for the blue since the species tends to be more solitary. Packs of mako are never encountered. All mako captures so far come from the western end of the English Channel or the northern part of the Bristol Channel.

Mako and porbeagle

The mako has so far not been recorded from Irish waters, while the porbeagle is widespread. Many parts of the coasts of the British Isles hold porbeagle with certain places in Wales and Scotland now producing specimens. So-called 'hot-spots' have been discovered off the Isle of Wight, North Cornwall, North Devon. But big catches may only be due to the great number of anglers fishing these areas. There are similar hot-spots off the west coast of Ireland.

If anglers concentrated on shark fishing many similar hot-spots would come to light, as has been proved in Shetland. Here, due to the effort of two anglers, many porbeagle have been hooked including two specimens. Comparison of the hot-spots shows that they have one factor in common. They are all tidal areas close or relatively close inshore often in association with reef areas or rough ground which are frequented by shoal fish such as herring or mackerel and to a very large extent pollack.

A similar distribution pattern appears to exist also for the thresher which may be encountered anywhere at any time around Britain. Again most records of capture come from the British south coast, but this probably only reflects the fact that there is more shark angling done in that part of our islands than elsewhere.

Mike Millman

Mike Millman

This rug is awarded by the Shark Angling Club of Great Britain to anglers who have caught shark of 250lb or more.

So far as the other species are concerned one, the Greenland shark, is definitely cold-water-loving so that the Shetlands would be the obvious place to expect the first rod-and-line capture. Perhaps some anglers fishing for common skate will be the first to catch one of these sharks. Since both the bramble and six-gilled sharks are bottom-dwelling species of rather deep water both could be taken anywhere angling is carried close to or in water of over 100 fathoms.

Of the British species which have been recorded as rod-and-line captures the six-gilled shark is the one with potentially the largest size. The present record, taken in 1976 off Penlee Point, Plymouth, at 9lb 8oz is no indication of the ultimate size for the species, for it is known to reach 1,500lb.

Even the British blue record of 218lb, a record which has stood since 1959, is no

indication of size for the world record is almost twice that weight. But fish of that size are uncommon and may become less so for the killing of these fish (especially by British anglers) means that there are fewer fish to reach the very big sizes. This is obvious when one considers the gradual decrease in size of the average weight of blue sharks taken off our south-west coast.

The world record weight of over 1,000lb for a mako may also be somewhat on the low side, for larger specimens are known. British anglers, therefore, still have a target to aim for, for the British record weight for the species of 500lb represents only 50% of the potential weight.

Cornwall's world record

So far as the porbeagle record is concerned, Britain heads the World list with the 465lb fish taken of Padstow, Cornwall in 1976. But commercial captures suggest that it may reach more than 600lb.

As with the blue and mako sharks, the British thresher record, established as long ago as 1933 off Dungeness, is no indication of ultimate size, for specimens in excess of 1,000lb, have been caught elsewhere, and have been sighted in our waters.

So far as the other species which have been mentioned are concerned, all with the exception of the bramble are giants, for while the latter probably does not go heavier than 300lb, hammerheads have been reported to 15ft and 1,000lb, while the tiger shark will probably reach twice that weight.

Legendary white shark

The weight and size of the white shark are legendary, with specimens in excess of 20ft and two tons having been caught in nets or by harpoon. These fish therefore make the world rod-caught record of 2,664lb taken off Australia look a little small.

In second place in the giant league must be placed the Greenland shark which in its cold waters reaches almost the same size as the white. It is an extremely sluggish species and is easily taken by hand-line and landed without any struggle. This is why it is also called the 'sleeper' shark.

Conger

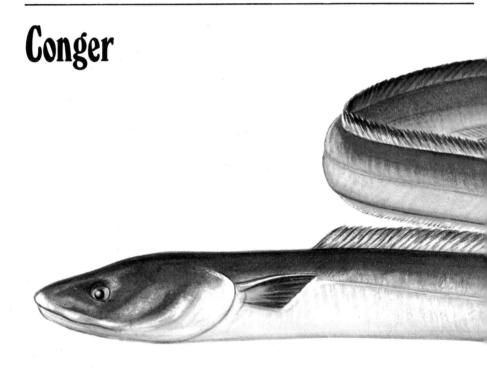

Research into the life cycle of the conger eel (*Conger conger*), has not been as thorough as that of other species. Only detailed research into sea species that are commercially useful has been carried out, and much of what has been written about the conger has yet to be proved. It does appear, though, that the conger eels seen in British coastal waters and caught by anglers are not in fact fully mature in spite of their large size. The British rod-caught record stands at 109lb 6oz, caught off Plymouth in 1976, but many larger fish have been recorded by British fishermen. There is evidence from deeper waters that the conger grows very much larger than was previously believed. In 1972 a fish of 220lb was taken in a trawl net off Denmark.

The conger is born in the ocean depths—spawning can take place as deep as 2,000 fathoms. Although it can only spawn once it is tremendously prolific, producing as many as 15 million eggs. These eggs are bathypelagic, they float freely in the sea at a great depth, and are carried on the slow-moving currents of the North Atlantic Drift towards the Continental Shelf. The larvae can take more than two years to reach the shallow coastal waters, and during that time they change, first to look like a narrow-headed leaf (leptocephalus) which is completely transparent and grows to a length of about 5in and then to the familiar cylindrical eel shape. These structural body changes (metamorphoses), are common in many fish species.

No mistaking the conger

The conger is first observed in British waters in the familiar eel shape and is sometimes mistaken for the common eel, but the differences are easy to spot. The dorsal fin on the conger starts level with its pectoral fins, that of the common eel starts much farther back along the body. The conger has scaleless skin and the upper jaw is longer than the lower one. The teeth are more pronounced in the conger and small congers stay mainly inshore and have a very

Distribution

Davis & Harrison VP Ltd

Habitat

The conger is found in deep water and inshore. It seeks wrecks, rocks, piles or harbour walls as hiding places. The rocky cove and small harbour at Dunquin, Co Kerry, Ireland (below) provides the perfect conger habitat.

Bait

Whole small fish, sides of large mackerel, the head and attached guts, all take conger.

Rod Sutterby

John Holden

Conger

(Left) A lively conger caught off Stromness, Orkney.
(Right) A mackerel head makes an attractive bait for conger.
(Far right) The British rod-caught record conger is 7ft 9½in long, has a girth of 2ft 5½in and weighs 109lb 6oz. Robin Potter hooked it over a wreck near the Eddystone reef in September 1976 and took 22 minutes to boat the giant fish.
(Below) Many charterboats have a well into which the conger can be dropped to avoid injury to anglers.

Bill Howes

Len Cacutt

fast growth rate. There is a well-authenticated case of a 3lb conger placed in Southport Aquarium and growing to 69lb in four years, and of another which reached 90lb in five and half years.

These smaller eels are voracious feeders, living on fish, lobsters, crabs and cuttlefish. They are not solitary fish, and tend to feed in groups. In the Bay of Biscay they have been observed hunting in packs when feeding on the octopus. When an octopus is found the group of congers will attack it and grip each of the octopus's tentacles in their powerful jaws, and spin backwards to dismember it and consume the remains.

The conger is found in the coast off the southern parts of Scandinavia, as far south as eastern Equatorial Africa, and the whole of the Mediterranean. Similar species can also be found on the Atlantic coast of America, the South Atlantic and the Indian and Pacific Oceans. As they grow in size, the majority retreat to deeper water, but many large fish live in convenient caves or holes close to a good food supply. Many harbours and fish quays have congers living close at hand, and some of them can grow very large indeed. Many of the very

large shore-caught conger have come from such places, one of the most notable being taken by Albert Lander at Torquay in 1967. This fish, which weighed 67¼lb, lived among some large pipes that had been lost overboard from a barge.

In other areas the conger retreats to deeper water during the day and moves inshore at night to feed. These fish are very susceptible to changes in water temperature, and a sudden very cold spell can kill them. Generally, during the colder weather, they retreat to the depths where the variation in temperature is very small.

Male conger do not grow as large as females, and although most standard re-

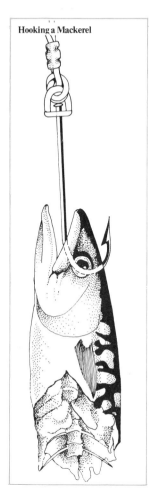

Hooking a Mackerel

Lyn Cawley

Mike Millman

ference books state that the male fish seldom exceeds 15lb, male fish have been caught weighing up to 35lb. The concensus of opinion seems to be that the male conger becomes sexually mature in about five years, but the female may take nearly ten years to develop. The conger dies before its eggs can become ripe. It would appear that the eggs need nearly a year to develop before they are fully ripe and the great depths of the ocean, with its tremendous water pressure, is a necessary factor for ripening.

If the conger is prevented from making this journey, by being kept in an aquarium for example, its body begins to change, it stops feeding, its bones become soft and its teeth fall out. The fish has adapted to a deep-water existence.

Where do conger spawn?

Unlike the common eel (*Anguilla anguilla*) there is no set time for the conger to migrate to their spawning grounds, but it is during the summer months, and although the spawning does take place in the Saragasso Sea region, the areas are never the same. It is possible that the conger has more than one area in which it spawns.

Large fish which are found inshore have already been mentioned, but the majority of big conger inhabit the deep water reefs and wrecks, and appear to be most prolific in the waters of the south and west coasts of this country. Certainly far more large congers are caught from these areas than from anywhere else, but it is possible that if the wrecks all around Britain's coast were fished equally large congers would be found.

The deep-water wrecks where the largest congers are found lie mostly on a seabed of mud or sand and give the appearance of large reefs rising from a featureless plain. The tidal currents run up channel, slacken off and then run down channel. During the tidal run many fish seek the shelter afforded by the wreckage. When the tide is at its strongest the conger bites are few, but as the tide slackens, fish begin to move around the wreck, and the congers emerge from their shelter and begin to feed.

The size of these fish is completely dependent on how much food is available, and the wrecks along the coasts of the West Country are living larders for the conger. Opinions vary as to just how often the larger fish do feed, but when wreck conger do start to feed they are very voracious and will take nearly any offering that is presented to them. Even when they have been hooked and broken free from a line, they till take another bait within a few minutes.

Conger tackle

The tackle used by the conger fisherman has to be adequate to cope with a very large and strong fish, but need not be of the 'broomstick' pattern. Many excellent conger have been caught on light tackle—what is needed is well balanced equipment and the patience to play the fish out thoroughly. A large conger can be winched to the surface before it has realized what is happening. Such a fish, full of fight on the surface of the water, is not a pleasant sight, especially to the person who has to gaff the fish and heave it on board.

Large congers thrashing about in a boat are very distracting and there are many theories as to the best way to quiet them. A heavy blow just above the vent can stun the fish, and a knife driven into the skull

between the eyes can kill it, but it is not always possible to get the fish into a suitable position to do either of these things. A heavy blow may miss the fish and do damage to tackle or to the floor boards of the boat. It seems that the best thing to do is either to transfer the fish to a box where it can remain unmolested or to throw a large sack or covering over the fish, when it will lie quietly.

Where conger feed

Although the conger is generally regarded as a bottom-living fish, feeding mainly on the seabed, this is not always true. There have been instances of conger being taken on baits fished in mid-water, and it is not uncommon to see a conger swimming on the surface in rocky inlets. The conger has its own method of avoiding the 'bends', the crippling result of the sudden change in water pressure that kills the majority of deep-water fish. As the conger rises to the surface it will belch, releasing air from its stomach and equalizing itself with the water pressure as it rises. The bubbles resulting from this action are often seen on the surface when a conger is hooked. This is one of the reasons why a conger can be so full of fight on the surface, whereas other species, such as the ling or pollack, are unable to return to the bottom.

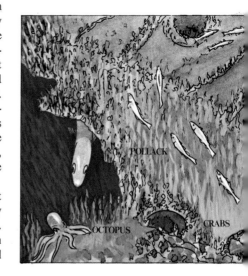

Mike Millman

(Above) A conger comes aboard. The gaff may look heavy compared with the size of the fish, but it avoids possible injury from the conger's extremely powerful jaws.
(Right) Conger diet includes crab, lobster and cuttlefish, but fish too are taken.

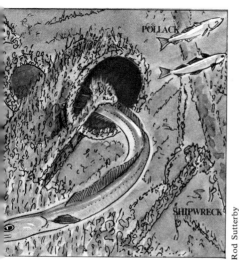

POLLACK

SHIPWRECK

Rod Sutterby

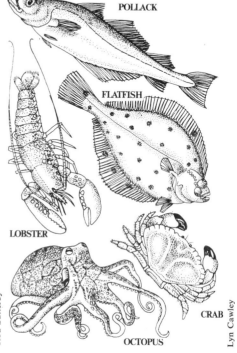

POLLACK

FLATFISH

LOBSTER

OCTOPUS

CRAB

Lyn Cawley

41

Mike Millman

Beachcasting rods

The first shorefishing tackle was a simple arrangement of hook, line and sinker either lowered into the sea from rocks and piers, or cast out with the aid of a pole. The line and pole are still used in parts of East Anglia and the West of Ireland. Roy Cook, a highly successful Suffolk beach fisherman, has updated the equipment to incorporate a line drum and winder which eliminate the laying out and retrieving of line by hand. He casts sinker and baits up to 140 yards, and the tackle is sensitive and powerful. For both bite detection and fighting big fish, however, the simple handline is superior to rods and reels.

At the turn of the century, shorefishing became a sport rather than the means of catching fish for the table. Rods were huge Burma canes or redundant salmon rods cut down at the tip. The emphasis was on strength. Crane-like designs continued to be employed until the late 1950s, although appearance and construction became more sophisticated. Even so the first glass-fibre rods retained the traditional weight and clumsiness that branded seafishing with its cloth-cap image.

Glass-fibre rods

Leslie Moncrieff's 'Springheel' rod heralded a new era of shorefishing, and was the first production beachcasting rod to exploit the advantages of glass-fibre. It became a huge success, not only because of the introduction of glass-fibre but because for the first time the average angler could expect to cast 100 yards. Moncrieff himself demonstrated that the rod, used with his 'Layback' casting style, would hurl 4oz and 6oz sinkers well beyond 150 yards—greatly in excess of contemporary tournament records. The effects on beachfishing were shattering—overnight the sport became highly technical and socially accepted.

The beachcasting tournaments became a battle-ground for designers and manufac-turers. A second breakthrough arrived in the form of ABU's 484, a stiff-butted rod with a very fast action that boosted casting range beyond the magical 200-yard barrier. Since then tournament distances have increased marginally to the current record cast of 222 yards, using a 6oz weight and a multiplier reel. Perhaps it is not a coincidence that as casters and rod-makers strive for extra performance, many shorefishing rods have become excellent casting implements but second-rate fishing tools. It was hoped that carbon-fibre would redress· the balance by giving maximum casting performance to

Roy Cook demonstrates his adaptation of the old handline and casting pole. The drum at the top of the pole stores the line, and a gear system is driven by the handle at the butt end. The cast is an over-the-shoulder throw, and Roy can cast an 11oz sinker and three cod baits well over 120 yards with this unusual rig.

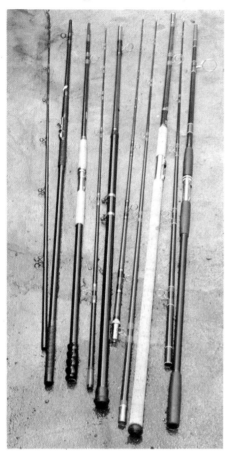

Bill Howes

(Left) A selection of beachcasting rods, available in many models and sizes.
(Below) Stand-off rod rings can be stainless steel, or have porcelain eyes.

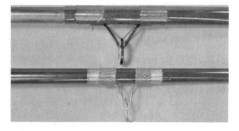

(Below) Top to bottom: plain and screwed metal ferrules an.. spiggot rod joints. They must be kept free from grit and sea water.

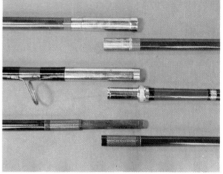

light, well-balanced rods that were still perfect for everyday fishing. So far the results are less than satisfactory, and the cost, at 10 times that of ordinary glass-fibre, is prohibitive. Nevertheless, the longer-term future of carbon-fibre is very bright indeed.

Rod construction

The construction of beachcasting rods follows a general pattern. A glass-fibre tube, the blank, is moulded around a cylindrical rod or mandrel, hardened; removed from the mandrel and ground smooth. It is cut and spigotted or ferruled to give two or three interlocking sections. The butt is sheathed in cork, sleeved with a plastic shrink tube or fitted with grips. Traditional winch fittings or simple sliding clips secure the reel. The rings, preferably• of stainless or hard-

chromed steel, plain or lined with ceramics, are whipped on in a combination of sizes and spacings so that the line foliows the curve of the blank. Handles, rings and other fittings, however, are almost irrelevant in terms of fishing performance except on very specialized rods. The heart of the rod is the blank, which determines power and action.

When selecting a rod the best guide is to choose the kind that is best suited to the fishing you propose to do. A rod for casting 6oz sinkers and hauling big fish through fast tides needs far more power than one used to catch flounders from quiet estuaries. Power in excess of the angler's physical strength is wasted, leading only to heaviness and severe handling problems. Most manufacturers recommend a sinker weight range for their products, and this may be taken as a fair estimate of the rod's power, but it is worth remembering that most rods are deliberately under-rated to insure against abuse. Many 4-6oz casting rods handle 8oz with ease. The only confirmation of a rod's suitability is to use it. If it suits your fishing without failing under pressure, it is adequate, provided that in casting you can bend it to its full curve.

The action, or how the rod responds to load, is controlled by the taper and wall thickness of the blank. A steeply tapered rod is faster than one which slopes gradually from butt to tip. Speed and action may be further enhanced by the process of compound tapering, a design where extra glass-fibre is applied at certain spots along the blank. Absolute rigidity of the butt may require the splicing on of high tensile Duralumin tubing. The merits of the various actions are debatable; there is no concensus among the world's top anglers as to which is best. Fast rods bend and flick straight in immediate response to casting and may improve distances with some styles, particularly tournament swings. They handle a wider range of sinker weights and are more sensitive to bites. On the other hand, slow rods cast far enough for fishing, are less sensitive to casting errors, and have a pleasant feel that many fast rods lack.

Rod length

Action alone is unlikely to affect practical fishing but does influence rod length, the most important criterion of all. A rod is a two-way lever which allows the angler to generate high sinker speed for long casting, yet magnifies the strength of a fish so that it seems to pull harder. Small fish seem much bigger on long rods,˙ and, although this makes for better sport, it leaves the angler at a disadvantage should he hook a monster. In addition, casting heavy sinkers becomes more difficult as rod length increases.

Overall length is related to action because the significant dimension is not the unflexed length but the distance from tip to butt when the rod is under full compression. Fast rods shorten dramatically as they bend, which

A beachcaster in action at Clew Bay, where many islands offer great beach fishing.

increases the mechanical advantage of the system. Casting is therefore easier than it might be with a slow rod to retain overall length under stress.

Rod length formulae are computed from the ratio between handle size and compressed tip length. The ratio is based upon the angler's physique, his casting style and the sinker weight he prefers. The first dimension to establish is handle size. The hands must be spaced roughly at shoulder width. Too far apart, and full power is impossible; too close, and casting is a considerable strain. As most anglers require a 25-30in handle, the ideal rod length for normal beachcasting to 150 yards range will be around 11ft for 4-6oz sinkers, and somewhat less for 6oz and above.

The usual process of increasing rod length in parallel with sinker weight is absurd, as simple physics will prove. In practice, the greater the weight, the shorter the rod. The average man casts 6oz further and more easily by exchanging his 12ft rod for one nearer 10ft. He also finds that the rod is lighter and better balanced, more fun to fish with, and less tiring when fighting a big fish.

Boat rods

Bill Howes

The sea angler's boat fishing rod is simply an extension to his arm. The rod acts as a lever, converting the pulling power of a handline to lifting strength. What has happened, over half a century or so, is that anglers have applied sporting techniques to the business of deep sea fishing.

Sea angling is probably the newest of the forms of angling. Certainly, fishing for really big fish only got underway at the turn of the century. Before that, it was easier, and possibly more productive, to use a hand or fixed line. Anglers went to sea as onlookers at the commercial fisherman's work. Showing an interest in the professionals' livelihood would gain anyone a place in the boat. They used handlines, so it was inevitable that the intending sport angler should follow suit. But a need grew to extend the sport beyond taking fish for the pot.

Beginning of sea angling

Sea angling was born. A knowledge of freshwater rods and the fact that they gave another dimension to the angler, that of introducing vibration, led to the production of sea rods in cane. These were clumsy compared with the modern glass-fibre equivalent, but they advanced sea fishing

considerably. At the time, it was believed that rods had to be strong. Rods were at first short because cane came in relatively short, useful lengths, and nobody wanted to introduce a metal or spliced join into the middle of them. Some had steel cores to give them further power for fighting big specimens. The expensive rod was made of split cane, with cheaper versions manufactured from whole cane sections often joined to whole wood handles.

Need for flexibility

Gradually it dawned on sea anglers that what was needed was a measure of flexibility. The ultra-strong, extremely stiff rod failed on two counts: it did not transmit the vibrations of a fighting fish to the angler at all well, neither could it flex to absorb a fish's wild rushes. Most of the movements of the fish resulted in a bending of the whole length of the rod. With the advent of extruded, solid glass rods, there was at last a material that could be relied on for bending freely; it rarely broke under pressure. This asset, however, was not a complete answer to the sea angler's prayers—solid glass bent under a load but did not have the recovery to the straight section that built cane had given. The material was cheap, so there was a flood of inexpensive rods on the angling market, and, although far from perfect in action, these brought fishing to many more people.

Controllable glass-fibre

The natural progression in the glass-fibre industry from drawing out glass fibres to weaving them into a cloth or mat was quick. Rod makers realized that they now had a material that could be controlled. There was enough demand for the more expensive rod for manufacturers to set up tube rolling plants. The Americans led for a number of years, but soon a British industry emerged. The simple technique involved impregnating a cloth, woven from glass fibres, rolling it around a steel mandrel to give it the shape and taper of the required blank, and then binding it tightly before placing the mandrel into an oven, where high temperatures set

the glass. After releasing the glass tube from the mandrel, the blank was then ground to produce a clean, even, smooth, tapered tube that produced a superb rod.

Action, the true requirement in the angler's boat rod, can be built into a rod in two ways. First, through the taper of the mandrel on which the glass-fibre is wrapped and, second, according to the amount of material used in a particular area of the rod. With these two factors settled, a curve of almost any power and compression can be put into the rod. There are differences in the type of glass and the resins that bind the whole thing together, but these have long been familiar to manufacturers.

Unbreakable

Glass-fibre rods are not only light and powerful; they are also almost unbreakable in sensible use. They are not affected by oil,

(Above left) A quiet moment during a deep sea angling session from a trawler off the North Devon coast near Appledore. A variety of rods is in use, mostly 6ft or 8ft long.
(Right) Boat rods come in a range of lengths and strengths depending upon the angler's choice.
(Below) For heavy duty deep sea fishing for powerful species, wire line is now popular. A roller tip ring bearing a stainless steel pulley is essential to avoid wear and grooving under friction.

Mike Prichard

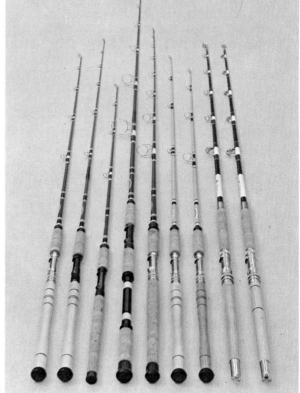

Frank Guttfield

Boat rods

saltwater and extremes of temperature. These features give the glass-fibre rod tremendous advantage over the older, more traditional rod-making materials.

No standard boat rod

There is no standard boat rod, nor can there be, for fish vary tremendously in size and the conditions under which they are fished for alter constantly. A rod of the 20lb class is suitable for small species in sea areas with light tidal flow and allows the use of light leads of 2–8oz. This means that the rod blank is balanced for use with a 20lb line. It will have a test curve of around 4lb, which means that a pull at the rod tip of this weight will bend the rod at right angles. It does not mean that the rod is only capable of handling a fish that weighs or pulls to 4lb. In any case, a fish weighs only about one third of its true weight when in the water. The test curve given for a sea rod is multiplied by five to arrive at the correct b.s. of line to match it.

Selecting a boat rod

When selecting a boat rod it is very misleading to wave it about in the manner usually adopted with freshwater rods, which do have a flexibility that can be assessed, even if not accurately. A boat rod only proves its worth under the stress of a sizeable fish coupled with the dead weight of a pound lead in a moderate tide.

A 30lb class rod will cope with fish up to 50lb, leads up to 20oz and quite hard tides—anything up to four or five knots—when fishing from an anchored boat. The rod is intended to be used for tope and big shoal fish such as cod, pollack, ling, and rays, but would still handle the smaller species. A 50lb class rod will enable anybody to hook, fight, and land most of our larger species. Porbeagle shark, all but the largest of common skate, and the average deep sea conger, all need a rod of this strength.

Skate and shark rods

Then there are the outlying fish—the huge common skate found off Shetland, Orkney and the West of Ireland and conger from the deep sea wrecks, where tides are fierce and the depth around 50 fathoms. This sort of

Bill Howes

(Above) Boat rods are built to withstand strains and stresses that would destroy coarse fishing equipment.
(Right) Three Hardy sea fishing rods for boat use. The centre rod carries a removable butt cap exposing a slotted gimbal fitting, used when a butt-pad is worn for heavy pumping.

fishing places a terrible stress on any rod, so the angler has to consider moving up to an 80lb class weapon. Big shark do not fall into this category because they are a free-moving species; the strain is caused by speed and a sustained fight rather than by a continuous, almost deadweight on the angler and rod.

The rod's fittings

No glass-fibre blank can perform as a rod without the right fittings. The quality of the glass and its design must be matched by a perfect winch fitting and rod rings. Ensure that the length of the handle is right for you, and remember that the winch fitting position is critical. Make sure too that you can reach the reel handle and control mechanisms. The choice of rings depends on the type of line that an angler prefers. Plain bridge rings are fine for use with monofilament nylon line but use at least a roller tip ring if the line is of braided Dacron or Terylene. There can be a lot of friction as these lines pass over the tip rings so a roller will help to reduce any friction. Remember, too, that saltwater is the enemy of any boat rod.

Boat rod lengths

Rods are becoming longer. At one time a 5 or 6ft rod was normal; now 7–8ft rods are commonplace. The longer rod gives better control of a fighting fish, especially when it comes close to the boat. At the same time it possesses more travel during compression, absorbing the wild lunges that can break a line when the angler is fishing with light tackle. There is a move, on the East Anglian coast, towards a fishing technique that requires a longer boat rod in order that the bait can be cast away at right angles across the tide. There is merit in the technique, although its practice requires considerable discipline from the fisherman.

Rod maintenance

The finish on a boat rod is not a complicated matter. Boat rods are subjected to knocks and hard usage that would soon destroy other fishing equipment. A seasonal rub down with a cleaning agent, followed by a gentle smoothing with 'wet and dry' sandpaper, will remove all the dross. It is then a matter of applying enough coats of polyurethane varnish to effectively seal the whipping on the rings and give the finish that the owner needs. Before varnishing, inspect the rings closely, looking for scuffing within the ring itself. Any ring that is worn must be replaced.

The best attention you can give to any rod used at sea is to wash it down after every trip with clean tap water.

Hardy's

Centrepin

Star drag

Winding handles

Palming rim

Mike Millman

The centrepin reel

Centrepin reels for sea fishing have a history stretching back into the middle eighteen hundreds. Early models were constructed from either teak, oak, or mahogony and had brass fittings. Most were about 4 inches in diameter and the narrow spools were capable of holding little more than 100 yards of the thick hemp lines common to the period. Gradually these lines gave way to much thinner plaited lines, which considerably increased the reel's capacity. A handle on either side of the drum was often too small and allowed little or no leverage. Before such refinements as check rachets and line guards were added, Nottingham and Scarborough reels were simplicity itself. Over the years centrepins manufactured from metal and

bakelite complemented the wooden varieties and, with little change in size or design they continued to be widely used for general sea fishing up to the late 1950's.

The technique for using a centrepin reel against heavy, fast running fish, such as pollack or bass, was not achieved easily. Anticipating the fish's behaviour and changing from winding to palming the drum, when the fish demanded line, required fine judgement. The inexperienced angler often suffered the penalty of cracked knuckles from flying handles or a monumental birds nest when the reel drum overran the line under pressure. This could lead all too often to the loss of a good fish. The author remembers, as an inexperienced angler, losing five double figure pollack in a row, during a trip off the

Bill Howes

Cornish coast, for one or other of the reasons mentioned.

Fishing with a centrepin without a slipping clutch, has the advantage of putting the angler in direct contact with the quarry. Every movement of the fish is instantly transmitted to the fingers, and once a level of experience has been gained, it is certainly one of the most sporting ways of fishing. Although the use of small centrepin reels declined with the introduction of the multiplier just after the Second World War, they are still used occasionally for boat fishing.

Centrepin's comeback

In the past few years there has been a slight swing back to centrepins, and a variety of new models are now available in tackle shops.

Large diameter centrepins for heavyweight species have long been popular and with good reason. Unlike the large modern multiplier, which is fished above the rod, thereby creating certain problems of balance, the centrepin hangs below and is really more comfortable to use when dealing with outsize fish such as shark, skate and conger. Line capacity is tremendous and most nine-inch reels can hold 600 yards of 60 to 80 lb braided line and considerably more monofilament. Of many excellent reels, one of the classics was undoubtedly Hardy's Fortuna, which went out of manufacture about twenty years ago. However there are still large numbers in everyday use aboard the sharking fleets running out of Cornish ports. The Fortuna, produced in a range of sizes from

Multiplier reels

MULTIPLIER (Saltwater)

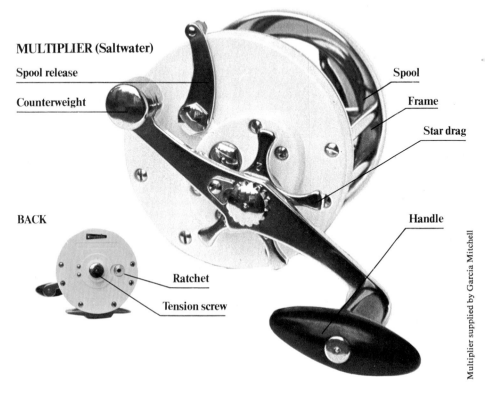

Spool release

Counterweight

Spool

Frame

Star drag

BACK

Handle

Ratchet

Tension screw

Multiplier supplied by Garcia Mitchell

12in down to 7in, featured a silk smooth movement and a clutch or star-drag that was second to none in positiveness and strength. The reels were fitted with two-inch handles which gave all the leverage one could wish for. The smallest Fortuna, and perhaps the most popular model, was the 7in weighing $5\frac{1}{2}$ lb. In mint condition the reel is a collectors item and can command a price in excess of £125. When new, every Fortuna came complete with a brass grease gun, which fitted five lubricating nipples on the back plate. Once heard, the sound of a Fortuna as line is ripped off it by a fast running fish is never forgotten. In every way it is a thoroughbred.

Centrepin technique

When fishing with a centrepin reel, it is vital

to set the drag light enough to allow a large fish to take line under pressure but when the time comes to strike or pump the fish it has to be tightened down allowing a safety margin in case of an unexpected run. If too much tension is used it is all too easy to tear the hook out of the fish's mouth.

The multiplier reel

The majority of boat anglers nowadays use the multiplying reel for fishing in both shallow and deep water. They range in size from 2/0 to 14/0, the latter being used to handle giant game fish. Multipliers are designed to retrieve line rapidly and have ratios between 2:1 and 5:1. In recent years, reels with automatic gearing have become popular. With a ratio range of $2\frac{1}{2}$:1 to $4\frac{1}{2}$:1 and in a few cases 5:1, they change down into low gear when a fish is pumped and up into a higher gear when only the line and terminal tackle is retrieved.

Another useful feature recently introduced is an inbuilt digital counter which accurately records and displays the footage of the line that is out. This can be very advantageous when fishing in deep water. Many multipliers have a rotating or bar-type line distributor which lays retrieved line evenly across the width of the spool.   All multipliers have either a star or lever drag which allows a fish to take line without the handles revolving. Star drags, which are cheaper to manufacture, vary considerable in their effectiveness. Cheap reels can strip after a period of time when used for deep water fishing against weighty specimens. It is always good policy to buy the best reel you can afford. Expensive reels incorporate what are described as aircraft quality bearings set in both end plates which gives the drum a smooth, even action and reduces friction to a minimum. Lever drag multipliers are more expensive but well worth the extra expenditure. The lever does away with the on/off mechanism necessary in conventional multipliers and allows the amount of drag imposed on a fish to be adjusted constantly throughout the time it is played. This can also be done with the star drag but not with as much ease or accuracy.

Multiplier technique

The technique of boat fishing with a multiplier is easily mastered. Provided one keeps a thumb on the spool as the weight runs to the bottom, few problems will be experienced. Failure to keep the free running spool in check can result in a birds nest. It is wrong to use the audible check as a means of controlling the spool or deliberately to tighten up the tension screw which controls distance between the flanges and side plates. Both of these methods result in considerable wear if not outright damage to the reel. Before loading a multiplier with nylon monofilament, a level of backing must be wound on to take the build up of pressure nylon imposes on the spool. Without it, the reel can literally burst apart during the playing of even a moderate size fish.

The use of wire line for deep water fishing, particularly where there is a fast run of tide, is rapidly gaining ground. It does, however, require quite distinct techniques and equipment.

Multipliers with wide spools and line levelers are quite unsuitable for use with wire which requires a narrow spool with good a line capacity. Whilst medium weight multipliers manufactured for boat use can be used for casting from the shore, there is an extensive range of reels designed specifically for the purpose featuring such refinements as spool tensioners and centrifugal breaking systems. These reels can be set to suit the casting weight by dialling a number on the back plate corresponding to the amount of lead being used. When this is cast, the drum revolves at just the right speed thus preventing a tangle. This can be a valuable asset when casting at night but one still needs a measure of practice to use the multiplier correctly in the dark.

The fixed spool reel

Fixed spool reels have a part to play in sea fishing from the shore. Since their introduction in the late 1930's, constant development has brought them to a high level of sophistication.

Development is still going on and fixed spools are giving way to skirted spools which are vastly superior in balance, smoothness movement and gearing. Long distances can be achieved with the lightest metal lures or natural baits, they are also suitable for float work from the shore or dinghy.

Large fixed spool reels with a line capacity of 250 yards and more of 25 lb breaking strain monofilament are used extensively for surf casting. These can handle large fish quite well but the wire bale arm is often distorted as the pressure is exerted on one side only. This type has a corrosion resistant finish, hardened, free running rollers and a very sturdy drag. Most wind on the left and the crank folds flat for easy fitting into a medium-size tackle box.

Braided lines

The perfect line, that will enable an angler to fish with every style and in any type of water, does not exist as yet. Developments in recent years have given a much greater range of lines to choose from and these include nylon monofilament, braided nylon, lead-cored, steel and the traditional silk line (now only found as a fly line for the dry fly purist). Naturally each of these lines has its uses, and although the vast majority are of monofilament, there is a strong case for braided lines with 'certain styles of fishing.

Manufacture

Braided lines are twisted from polester fibre, a synthetic substance manufactured from raw materials which include coal, water and petroleum. It is the petroleum ingredient that in part accounts for the steady rise in price of this line over the past few years. Like monofilament, the polyester fibre is extruded under pressure, but any similarity ends here.

Braided lines are soft, pliable, and can be purchased in continuous lengths of up to 1,000 yards. Unlike monofilament, however, the line is not translucent. Nor is it now manufactured in breaking strains of less than 10lb—a great loss to the angling world. In the sizes sold, its circumference is greater than that of monofilament, and it naturally follows that less line can be wound onto a normal reel. This is a disadvantage.

Braided line possesses numerous advantages, not least its complete lack of spring. This makes it easy to wind from the spool onto the reel. it knots easily, the knots pulling firmly together without slipping,

Mike Millman

54

and, naturally, this makes for greater security. Regardless of the material, there must be some loss of strength with every knot that is tied, but the seriousness of this is much less acute with a braided line. The lines are hardly affected by water and have a high resistance to sunlight, mildew and rot, needing only an occasional wipe with a soft cloth to remove fine particles of grit that act as an abrasive on fishing lines.

The stretch problem

Every angler who has tried to pull his hook free from a snag will vouch for the fact that monofilament line stretches astronomically under pressure. In fact, it stretches by 17 to 80 per cent, depending on its method of manufacture. Over-stretching leads to distortion in the line's shape, and causes permanent weakness, often over considerable distances. In use, the braided line will only stretch a maximum of 10 per cent, and only does this in the period immediately before breaking occurs. Thus the risk of permanent damage is small.

This almost complete lack of stretch is a great help in preventing line from jamming on the spool of your reel, where a direct pull with monofilament line can often force one strand under others below it and bring the whole reel to a halt.

Undoubtedly, it is the stretch factor that had endeared the braided line to anglers who need a strong and reliable line for really hard work—work which includes spinning, trolling and heavy sea fishing where the extra bulk needed to accommodate the thicker line can be found in the large reels used, and where continued pulling against snagged terminal tackle will cause little or no risk of future line weakness.

While the initial outlay may cause many anglers to think twice before purchasing a braided line, there is a strong case for its use as a longterm money-saver.

(Left) A shark reel loaded with braided line.
(Right) The line in action.
(Below) The structure of 130lb b.s. braided line.

Bill Howes

BRAIDED LINE

Rod Sutterby

Wire lines

The relatively recent introduction of wire line for boat fishing has been the most important sea angling innovation of the century. It was first introduced to this country from America a little over 10 years ago, and that great sea angler Leslie Moncrieff was one of the first fishermen over here to use and popularize it. It was first developed in the States to allow big-game anglers to troll baits without the encumbrance of a heavy lead, and while it is still used over there for this purpose, it is now also used extensively in conjunction with lead or a down-rigger for slow trolling at depths of up to 100ft for salmon and lake trout in freshwater.

It was quickly realized by sea anglers in this country that here was the answer to bottom fishing in strong tides or deep water. In fact it exceeded all expectations once the correct techniques for using it had been perfected and some incredible bags of fish were taken by boat fishermen where other anglers using conventional lines had very indifferent results.

Acceptance only a matter of time

So far, fishing with wire line has still to be accepted by the average sea angler, although it is surely only a matter of time before this happens. Fishing with wire requires completely different techniques and equipment, but it is not difficult to learn. With a little practice, the average angler can become proficient in its use in a comparatively short time. Unfortunately, in the early days it quickly received a bad reputation as many anglers, using it as just another fishing line, had disastrous results.

The original wire also was of a single strand construction from Monel metal and considerable developments and improvements have been made since that was first marketed. While the single-strand wire was very hard wearing and less prone to kinking, it was much thicker than more recent lines

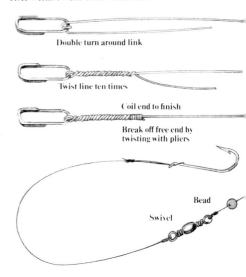

HAYWIRE TWIST FOR WIRE LINE

Double turn around link

Twist line ten times

Coil end to finish

Break off free end by twisting with pliers

Bead

Swivel

and rather unpleasant to use. It was followed by a single strand, stainless line which was beautiful to use but very prone to kinking, and these kinks, once formed, were all but impossible to remove.

In efforts to overcome this problem, a very flexible seven-strand wire was evolved, and while this format succeeded to some extent, the multiple stranding produced a further problem. With constant use, some of the strands were liable to fracture and where this happened, badly lacerated fingers were often the result. Apart from this, it was found in practice that salt water badly affected stainless wire over a period of time and its strength rapidly deteriorated.

The latest wire to appear on the market has a chrome base; it is very soft, pleasant to use, resistant to kinking and completely unaffected by salt water, so it overcomes most of the problems which gave wire lines a poor reputation. The name of this new line is 'Tidebeater' (supplied by Efgeeco), and it is the only wire line now being manufactured and currently offered for sale in the U.K.

(Right) The ideal reels for wire line are the very large-diameter kinds such as this huge wooden starback centre-pin.

WIRE LINE RIG

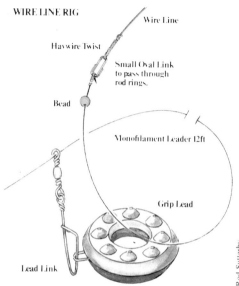

Wire Line

Haywire Twist

Small Oval Link to pass through rod rings.

Bead

Monofilament Leader 12ft

Grip Lead

Lead Link

Rod Sutterby

Bill Howes

Used correctly, wire line can open up a new world to the sea angler. To hold bottom, you require a fraction of the lead compared with conventional monofilament or braided lines of Dacron or Terylene. In very strong tides, for example, and fairly deep water where you would require at least 2lb of lead on a monofilament line to hold bottom, you can achieve the same result using wire with less than ½lb. This means you are in closer touch with the fish at all times, and it is far more sporting, as, after all, the average-size sea fish of 6–7lb can hardly give of its best when it is towing a large, heavy lead.

Bite indication

Bite indication with wire is a revelation in itself: bites from small fish are registered immediately and positively, where similar bites on monofilament would not be felt at all, due to its inherent stretch. So positive is the indication from wire line that an angler experienced in its use can, even in deep water, tell you the composition of the bottom –whether it is rock, sand, shingle or soft mud –just from the feel of the bouncing lead.

The one disadvantage of wire line is that fishing from a crowded boat becomes in-advisable. When using wire you require plenty of room between you and the next angler, as it is absolutely essential to keep wire under tension at all times, and should you become entangled with another fisherman's line this is not possible. Wire reverts to coil form when tension is relaxed, and most efforts to straighten it result in kinks, so that it then becomes so weak that it will snap under the slightest pressure.

This brings us to the first and most important aspect of its use, and the one that causes most problems to novices. Never, *never* lower weighted wire to the bottom from a free spool, as if you do you will not know when the lead hits the seabed. The result will be a pyramid of coiled wire on the bottom which will come back full of kinks. Lower it under slight tension, with your thumb on the spool of the reel and you will then feel the lead arrive.

When using wire it is advisable to mount your running lead on a heavy monofilament

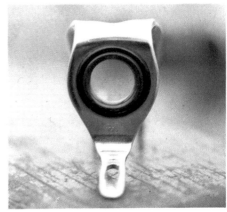

leader at least 12ft long. This should be fastened to a small, oval link or split ring that is small enough to be wound through the rod guides and down onto the reel. It will mean, in effect, that when your lead with its normal flowing trace is wound in, all the wire will be back on the spool.

If you neglect to do this and mount your lead directly onto the wire, it will be left to swing like a pendulum from your rod top when moving from one anchorage to another, and this constant motion will cause metal fatigue with corresponding weakness in the line. Wire should always be connected to the metal loop or split ring with a haywire twist. But be sure to take a double loop through the ring before commencing the twist.

A heavy leader serves another purpose in as much as it provides a small degree of stretch between the angler and a heavy fish. Without this cushioning effect, it is all too easy to tear the hook free.

The tackle required for wire is a reel with a large diameter, yet narrow, spool such as a Scarborough, Alvey or, ideally, a Penn Master Mariner. Normal multiplying reels with wide, small diameter spools are useless as these coil the line too tightly and it will then require a heavy lead to straighten it. For the same reason, you should use a rod with a soft action and flexible top, and it is absolutely essential that it is fitted with a roller top or better still, roller guides all the way down the rod. ·

(Above left) A roller-type intermediate ring for wire-line fishing.
(Above) New-type boat ring by Fuji with an aluminium oxide guide for wire fishing.
(Below) Ordinary ring damaged by wire line.

Finally, one word of warning to those fishing from an anchored boat, or more especially from a drifting boat. Never attempt to free wire with your hands should it become snagged on the bottom. It can cut through flesh like a hot knife through butter. Loop the line round a stanchion or stem post, and let the boat pull it out. It is also sound practice to use a trace of slightly lower breaking strain than the wire so that if you do have to break out, you will only lose a hook or part of the trace and not many yards of relatively expensive wire.

Sea hooks

No item of the sea angler's equipment is more important than the hook which, after all, is in direct contact with the fish and so has to withstand all kinds of strain.

Despite this, hooks often receive scant attention. Many anglers will cheerfully part with £60 for a rod, reel and line, and then go out of their way to buy cheap hooks, which are brittle, poorly finished and often quite unsuited to the job they are expected to do. Others purchase good hooks, but then allow them to become rusty and blunt, with points that will hardly penetrate the softest mouth.

Hook manufacture

Before we look at the most popular hooks for sea fishing, it is as well to examine the method of manufacture that produces a good hook. Most are made from high-carbon steel wire. One machine straightens the wire from a large coil and a second cuts it to the appropriate length. The 'needles' obtained from this operation are then ground to a rough point, and another grinding imparts a fine hollow-ground point. The blunt-end of the shank may now be 'pennelled' or tapered by grinding, which allows the eye to be closed up smaller.

A steel chisel cuts a barb in the needles as they move round a rotating drum, the angle and the depth of the incision being determined by the setting of the chisel. Different fishing methods call for this variety of barb.

The next step is bending, which is carried out round a mandrel or cylinder. Variations on the angle of the bend are numerous, and each style of hook and size has its own.

The eye is now formed. It is either left straight or can be set towards or away from the point. Some hooks, for example, those used in mackerel fishing, are flattened in the shank, while others have grooves for whipping on flies or feathers. For extra strength, large hooks can be brazed, as are the Mustad Seamaster range, which are used

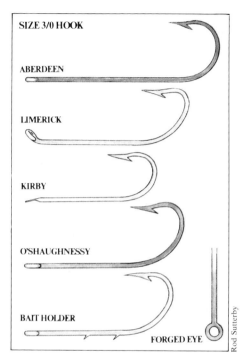

SIZE 3/0 HOOK

ABERDEEN

LIMERICK

KIRBY

O'SHAUGHNESSY

BAIT HOLDER

FORGED EYE

Rod Sutterby

for shark and game fishing throughout the world. This kind of hook is also subjected to anti-corrosion tests in a salt spray chamber in accordance with internationally agreed standards. To minimize corrosion, hooks are plated with either bronze, tin, nickel or even as has been known, gold.

Hook size

Treble hooks, which are now wisely used for pirk fishing over deep-water wrecks, are also brazed. As much of the work is done by hand, the cost can be considerable. Hardening and tempering by heating, and then cooling with oil, give maximum strength and resilience. Finally the hooks are scoured in revolving drums filled with an abrasive, and then polished in a similar way with a mixture of sawdust and oil. These operations together produce a hook that can be relied on to perform perfectly.

A fair proportion of anglers are confused

BRITISH [REDDITCH] HOOK SCALE

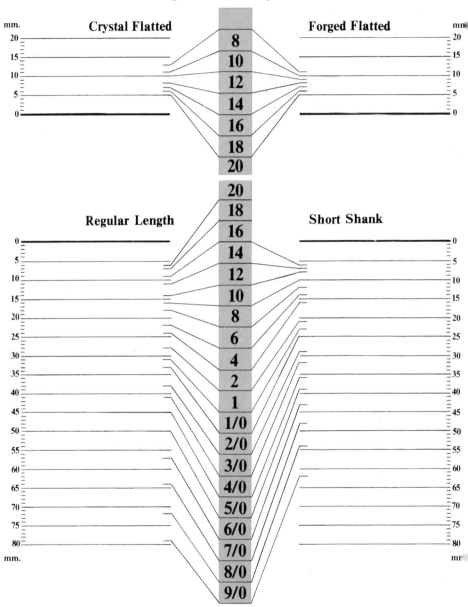

Our chart is based on the Sealey-Redditch Hook Scale. By using it you can easily determine the overall length and the size of a hook when this is not known. The hook's length in millimetres is in direct relation to the size scale in the central column.

D. C. Edwards

60

by the multiplicity of hook sizes, which largely stems from the traditional use of private scales. The world's fish hook manufacturers now use only the British (Redditch) scale.

Hook style

So much for hook manufacture and sizes. This still leaves the bewildering array of styles of hook. For sea fishing this can be reduced conveniently to around half a dozen kinds. Among the most popular is the razor sharp, straight eyed Aberdeen hook which has a long shank made from light wire. Perfect temper prevents any straightening despite the extra leverage from the shank. This hook is used extensively for estuary fishing, particularly for bass, plaice and flounders. As it is so fine in the shank of wire the Aberdeen is most suitable for baiting live sandeel and prawn.

Shore anglers who fish from the precipitous rock ledges of the north Cornwall coast also swear by them for spinning with

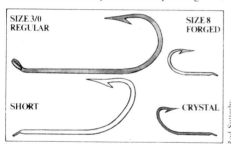

deadbaits for fast-moving mackerel, garfish, pollack and bass. Some will argue that it is the only hook for saltwater fishing. That is a bit sweeping, but every self-respecting sea fisherman should be equipped with a range of Aberdeens between the sizes No.1 and 4/0, with the emphasis on No.3/0.

For general bottom fishing three kinds stand out—Limerick, Kirby and O'Shaughnessy. The Limerick is well suited to use with a paternoster for bream, whiting, pouting, cod and ling, its pull being direct and its penetration excellent. For ledgering there is little to choose between the other varieties, which have a wide gape between

the point and the shank, but the O'Shaughnessy is the strongest and particularly suitable for holding conger eel.

The conger is a fish that demands and receives respect from beginner and expert alike. In the past decade the development of deep-water wreck fishing has produced some enormous congers, some over 100lb in weight. To cope with the strength and sawing motion of the conger's jaws and to withstand prolonged battles, a hook must be durable, and this is where the forged eye hook comes into its own. In conger fishing for the big specimens, finesse goes out of the window. Eels over 50lb have a large appetite, and the experts think little of offering a whole bream weighing as much as 3lb. Such a bait, intended to attract huge fish, requires a forged hook of either No.10/0 or 12/0 attached to a couple of feet of cable-laid wire. No matter how much pressure this kind of hook receives, it will not straighten out as a conventional conger hook may well do.

Another hook that has become a favourite in recent years is the 'bait holder', which is designed with two slices in the shank to prevent the bait slipping down to the bend. The design has its disadvantages, though, as the wire needs to be thick, penetration is only average, and worm baits are literally ripped to pieces by the sharp edges. Worst of all, the nicks in the shank reduce the strength of the metal by at least 50 per cent.

Care of hooks

No article on hooks would be complete without reference to the care of them. While most are sharp when they leave the factory, handling can easily dull them, and so it is essential to examine each one before it is used, and from time to time while fishing. Any with a slightly turned point and those lacking needle sharpness should be gently honed with a good stone. Soft Arkansas whetstone, used with a light oil, is perfect for the job. Hooks that show signs of irreparable wear must be discarded after each trip. Failure to observe this simple rule could lose you the fish of a lifetime.

Sea leads

Split Shot

Ball Leads (Pierced Bullets)

Barrel Lead

Flat Leads (Coffin or Ledger Leads)

Circular Grip

Capta Lead

6 Pointed Star

Leads for sea angling range from split-shot to bombs weighing as much as 4lb which keep a bait on the bottom in deep water during fierce spring tides. There are many different types and each performs a specific task. With a few exceptions, it is of paramount importance to use the right shape and size of weight for the type of fishing being undertaken.

Shore fishing

Split-shot, the indispensable lead used in freshwater fishing, also plays a vital role in saltwater, where it is used in float fishing and drift-lining for such species as pollack, mackerel, garfish and the wily mullet. Shot is available in a variety of sizes, and should be gently crimped onto the line with pliers.

Ball leads (also known as pierced bullets) and barrel leads, which are designed to run freely on a line, range from $\frac{1}{4}$oz to 3oz. These leads are correct for making up the sliding float rig used to suspend a bait close to the bottom in almost any depth of water. The 'slider' is popular with anglers seeking wrasse, pollack and bass over rough ground. Barrel leads weighing up to 6oz are sold in many tackle shops for bottom ledgering, but they roll around on firm sandy ground, and tend to twist the line. These larger sizes, therefore, make a poor type of lead and are best avoided.

Leads for muddy ground

For ledgering on muddy ground in tidal rivers and estuaries where the water is shallow, flat leads are by far the best. Although they make for poor long-distance casting, those with a thin profile sink to the bottom more slowly than bombs and consequently do not penetrate more than a few inches into the ooze. Extensions of the smooth, flat weight are the Circular Grip, Capta and the Six Pointed Star. These are useless as casting leads, but they hold well on firm mud, shale and sand—even when the tide pours out of rivers during spring tides.

(Left) Beachcasting: the shape and weight of lead selected is important.

The long-casting beach angler needs a variety of weights ranging in size from 2oz to 10oz, which offer minimum wind-resistance. Across the years numerous patterns have evolved, and present day beach fishing experts think little of putting an intact bait 160 yards out into the surf where the big fish roam. A small band of men who specialize in this fascinating branch of sea sport, using carbon-fibre rods, are already casting way beyond 225 yards and, as this material becomes even more sophisticated, 300 yards may well fall within the range of normal beachcasting as opposed to tournament casting.

The long-distance lead

Aerodynamically, the Arlesey bomb is the best lead for reaching these great distances. A swivel at the narrow end stops the reel line twisting during its flight, but once on the sea bed it is a poor holder and is easily rolled around by water movement. The compromise is a Torpedo with four flat sides and with its weight concentrated at the pointed end, which prevents the lead turning over in flight. From this lead came the Spiked Torpedo, featuring four or more soft wire arms embedded in the heavy end. These dig into the sand and prevent the lead from moving in all but the·roughest weather. Under retrieving pressure,·however, the arms bend backwards and the lead can be wound in easily.

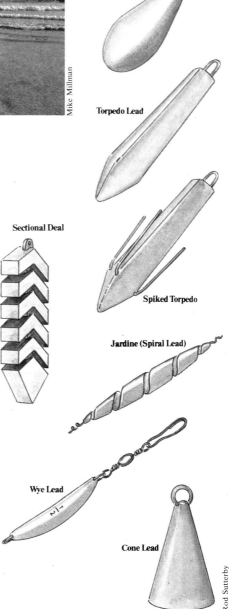

Arlesey Bomb

Torpedo Lead

Sectional Deal

Spiked Torpedo

Jardine (Spiral Lead)

Wye Lead

Cone Lead

Sea leads

Mike Millman

Although similar in appearance to the normal Torpedo, the Sectional Deal beach lead is made up from five 2oz pieces, moulded in a V-shape, which fit together on a central bar, fastened into a pointed bottom section of 4oz. Each piece simply lifts off the bar—giving six casting weights in one.

For spinning from the shore, the weight must hug the line and present the minimum resistance to air and to water. A spiral like the Jardine takes a lot of beating. It has a continuous groove running from end to end, and twisted wires through which the line is passed. Jardines come in weights from 2oz to 8oz, the lighter versions being the most suitable for general spinning work with natural and artificial sandeel or fish-strip baits. The banana-shaped Wye lead, fitted with a link swivel, is also excellent for spinning. As with the Jardine, nothing should be placed on the line between the lead and bait. Both these types are suitable for working ultra-light metal lures, or for increasing range with heavier models.

Leads for boat fishing

It is possible to break down boat fishing into four categories: inshore, offshore, pirking and trolling. Many types of lead and many different techniques used in shore fishing have a use when working from a boat in shallow water. Float work is exactly the same, but for drift-lining when the boat is anchored in a fair run of tide, the weight must be increased to get the bait down below the surface. Two- or three-hook paternosters can be weighted with Arlesey bombs, plain bombs or small Torpedoes. For ledgering, use Cones, Circular Grip and Star types.

Offshore fishing

In offshore fishing the angler meets with the combination of deep and swift-running water, particularly during spring tide periods. The type of reel line is a most important factor when fishing in more than 20 fathoms. Monofilament creates much less drag than braided line, and less weight is needed. From an anchored boat, a 4–5 knot run of tide will push a 1lb lead connected to braided line almost to the surface. When this occurs, the lead will be some 300 yards away, down tide.

In water 35–45 fathoms deep it is impossible during spring tides to keep 3lb of lead on the bottom. This is one reason why charter skippers always drift-fish during new and full moon periods. It is as well to remember this when booking a deep-water

Irish Tourist Board

fishing trip; working 'on the drift' can be a hard, tiring business.

Paternosters can be made to sink with bombs or torpedoes, and it is wise to have a range from 6oz to 2lb with you even when the tide is a neap. The same types are used in association with wire boom rigs for long-trace, single-hook fishing. Rarely, however, do you need more than 10oz when this method is used as the bait is fished up to 60ft above the bottom.

Deep-water leads

Leads for ledgering in deep water must have a large diameter base. The cone is the best type, but grip leads do an adequate job. Ledger leads can be rigged with a 'rotten bottom' by tying a small swivel to the eye with light nylon. If the weight gets caught up in a rock crevice or a wreck, steady pulling will free the trace end. This is a big comfort when expensive wire traces are in use.

Trolling for bass and pollack is a popular and often rewarding way of fishing. The size of the lead depends very much on the strength of tide, speed of the boat and how deep the fish are running. For deep work 1lb is about right, and for shallow fishing 8–12oz should be used. Trolling leads should have a centre of gravity below the level of the line. This prevents any suggestion of spinning—providing, of course, that the swivels mounted behind and in front of the weight are in working order. Large Jardines rigged in the manner described earlier are also widely used and can be changed very quickly, without cutting the reel line, should a heavier or lighter one be needed.

Factory-made leads are now very expensive. The average 8oz weight costs at least 22p and a 2lb bomb will set you back 70p. The alternative is to buy die-cast aluminium moulds and lead from a scrap metal dealer and to make your own. The initial outlay for a set of moulds to make 2oz, 3oz, 4oz, 5oz, 6oz and 8oz weights plus a bag of grip wires will be about £12—but of course you can start with a single block and gradually build up the range. The price of lead varies from week to week; a modest fiver will get you enough to make several dozen leads of various sizes and, certainly, the unit cost is less than half the shop price. Over a period of time it is a worthwhile proposition.

Home-made leads

Lead weight making should be done in a shed—never in a kitchen. Unless approached correctly it is a dangerous business, and children must be kept well away from the operation. Lead pipe should be cut up into small pieces and melted in an iron ladle over a paraffin or gas blow lamp. When ready for use the metal is poured slowly into the block which should be gripped lightly in a vice. Moulds must be absolutely dry before use or the molten metal will spit in all directions when it strikes the aluminium—with tragic results. After allowing a few minutes for the casts to set, the mould can be removed, split open and the lead dropped to one side. After a dozen or so leads have been fashioned the block becomes very hot and must be left to cool for at least ten minutes. Needless to say, gloves should always be worn throughout.

(Above left) Jardine leads are probably the best shape for sea spinning from rocks or the shore.
(Left) A small codling taken on a simple trace and bomb-shaped lead.
(Right) A box of large leads made for a week's exciting charter-fishing in the Plymouth area.

Len Cacutt

Sea swivels

One of the most useful, but most neglected accessories for the angler is the swivel. It is primarily used to prevent fishing line from becoming twisted, and whether the angler employs any of the various forms of spinning, or merely retrieves a deadbait, the turning action of the bait spiralling through the water will be transferred to the line. If monofilament is allowed to twist, it begins to kink, and at best becomes a tangled mess—at worst the line weakens so badly that it will break at the first strain.

The only preventative is the use of one or more efficient swivels mounted between the line and lure, working in conjunction with an anti-kink weight or vane. Such devices are attached to the reel line by means of a bloodknot or grinner knot. But efficiency is difficult to achieve in a swivel. Early traces had two, three or more swivels, operating on the principle that the more that were added, the better the chance of at least one working. Those early mechanisms were in the form of an open, oblong box with eyes mounted through each end. A little corrosion or rust plus an accumulation of grit and mud quickly impaired their efficiency.

One basic principle

Today, the angler has the choice of several types of swivel, all working on the same basic principle but with varying refinements. The plain barrel swivel is the most popular and probably the tackle dealer's best seller especially since many anglers simply ask for 'a swivel' and leave the choice to the assistant. Its construction is simple, with two eyes (through which trace and line are mounted) allowed to revolve independently on their separate beads of metal carefully shaped to fit the inside of the barrel. The free rotation of the eyes depends on tolerances left when the thin metal is compressed during machining: nine times out of ten, the tolerances are adequate and the swivel revolves freely. The tenth case is where

trouble sets in, and before leaving the shop it is worth checking each swivel that is purchased, and again before fishing.

An improvement on the plain barrel is the American Berkley swivel. It differs only in that a good grade of metal is used and the eyes are flattened slightly at the terminal ends to ensure that trace and line stay in place, free from a natural tendency to pull to either side when an unequal strain is applied. An improvement in efficiency which costs little more, is the Hardy Ball Bearing swivel. Again, there is the barrel type of construction but with exacting tolerances and incorporating small ball-races that ensure that the eyed pieces revolve freely.

One swivel remains in this category—the Diamond swivel, in which the loops are not round but diamond-shaped and are fastened by means of an expanded link. Usually

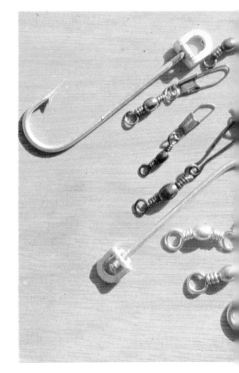

manufactured from fine steel, they appear rather flimsy, but in fact are equal in strength to other types. They are considerably lighter and rarely jam.

Swivels for freshwater fishing are usually made of brass or blued steel. However, these materials are not strong enough to withstand the strains placed upon them by the rigours of saltwater fishing. For this reason the usual material for swivels for the heavier forms of sea fishing is stainless steel as it is not only tougher and more resistant to bending, but is also not attacked by saltwater, even so they should be checked at regular intervals.

Sea water is very abrasive too, because of the particles of sand suspended in it, so the rather open construction of a barrel swivel will allow sand to enter and cause damage to the moving parts. This is not very important if the swivels are bought cheaply and thrown away after use, as is often the case with sea anglers who fish for the smaller, weaker species around our coastline, so that it is not too serious if a swivel jams.

SWIVELS AND LINKS

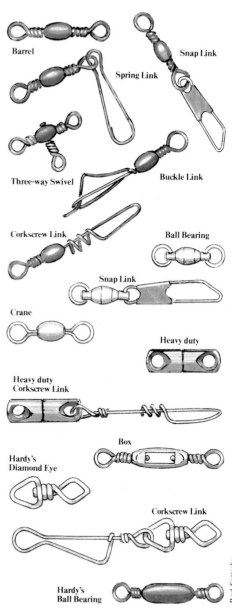

Mike Millman

Rod Sutterby

(Above) There is a wide variety of swivels available to the angler, catering for the demands of different waters and species. (Left) A selection of the swivels and booms needed by the sea angler if he is to cope with the sea's powerful fishes.

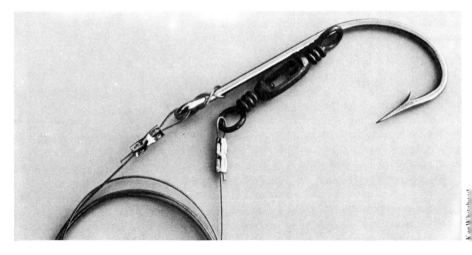

Matters can be very different if you are fishing for big conger eels, skate, or shark, and the angler who is lucky enough to fish for such hard-fighting, powerful species as marlin, or broadbill swordfish, or the very biggest sharks, should never use anything but the very best tackle, including swivels which are engineering marvels.

These swivels will be made of stainless steel or a really hard alloy not affected by sea water. All moving parts will be machined to very fine tolerances, so that it is almost impossible for abrasive particles to enter and will probably be grease-filled as a further protection. Miniature ball-races can be built in to ensure the smoothest possible rotation by minimizing friction, and modern developments have produced swivels which are far in advance of the simple barrel-type device.

One kind of swivel stands on its own, and that is the three-way swivel which is most frequently used in forming the float paternoster for fishing a livebait. Constructed in the barrel style with an extension eye standing out from its side, it is prone to distortion and weakness if the bait gets caught and extreme pressure is applied as the angler pulls to break free. The only precaution against this weakness is to recognize it and replace the swivel immediately.

Link swivels are a means of quickly attaching (or detaching) a lure to a trace, or to a line. Ideally they should be simple to open and close—even with wet, cold hands—and strong enough to grip without collapsing when extreme pressure is applied.

Plain link swivels with two overlapping half-clips seem to find greatest favour among anglers, despite the fact that they are difficult to open when needed and often slip open without warning to shed either lure or trace during use. An improvement is the safety-pin link, where an open steel loop doubles back to fasten—as the name suggests—into a metal clip. Providing the clip is secure and there is sufficient overlap on the pin to fit snugly into it, this is a safer and more convenient unit than the plain link.

At first sight the diamond-link looks a flimsy affair of a single wire loop doubling back to clip over itself. But in practice it is strong, simple and easy to clean.

How many swivels to use?

How many swivels should be used when fishing? Generally, the fewer the better: every swivel requires a join either to the line or cast, which weakens it. On most occasions just one is enough, provided that it has been properly maintained and is used with an efficient anti-kink vane. But there are arguable exceptions to this rule. Some would say that the choice depends upon the length of the trace: a short trace needing two swivels, one at each end. A longer trace needs a third.

Sea booms

To the expert, the array of terminal tackle displayed in the sea section of a tackle shop is fascinating; but for the beginner or inexperienced angler that same array can be a nightmare of odd-shaped wire lengths. Terminal tackle for sea fishing has certainly undergone many changes in recent years, and the mixing of old and new, coupled with the barriers created when various items are identified by different names in different parts of the country, often leads to misunderstandings. Nevertheless, if the angler remembers his basic fish lore, selecting the right tackle is common sense.

Importance of swivels

Most sea tackle is designed for quick release, so that lead or reel line can be altered with the minimum of disturbance and, to counter the twisting action of the sea, swivels should be incorporated wherever possible. Because there is a tendency for hooks and line to twine together, wire, in the form of a boom, is used to keep the bait away from the reel line, and as snag-free as possible. The size of the boom and its position depend on the depth at which the bait will be presented, which in turn depends on where the fish sought are believed to be feeding.

The most popular item of end tackle is probably the paternoster. This is an arrangement of wire arms that will hold hooks at right-angles to the line both on and just above the sea bed, making it ideal for use over uneven ground. There are two and three-boomed varieties, the booms being spread out and held by the terminal weight, which is attached by a corkscrew link. The material used for paternosters is usually brass, but stainless steel, giving a firmer, more subtle arrangement, has found favour with many anglers, especially in the early part of the season when the water is clear.

Efficiency with the metal paternoster is at its best when the line is held vertically, with the rod tip above it, and this, in the vast

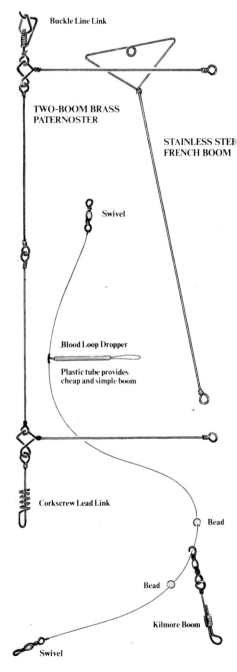

Buckle Line Link

TWO-BOOM BRASS PATERNOSTER

STAINLESS STEEl FRENCH BOOM

Swivel

Blood Loop Dropper

Plastic tube provides cheap and simple boom

Corkscrew Lead Link

Bead

Bead

Kilmore Boom

Swivel

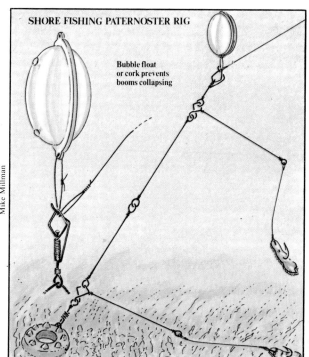

SHORE FISHING PATERNOSTER RIG

Bubble float
or cork prevents
booms collapsing

Mike Millman

Rod Sutterby

*(Above) A pollack rig based on a French boom, 20ft trace and artificial eel.
(Left) A two-boom brass paternoster, stainless steel French boom, and the useful Wessex ledger.
(Right) A bubble float or cork aids bait presentation.*

majority of cases, means fishing from a boat. When the rig is used for shore fishing, the lack of angle between line and the bottom will cause the booms to collapse. To prevent this happening, some anglers fix a large bubble float or piece of cork above the buckle swivel where the reel line is attached, which lifts the rig into a vertical position.

French booms

The ready-made paternoster presents the hook only 2ft or so above the bottom. Where it is required to hold a bait well above the sea bed, French booms should be used. These triangular wire frames can be fastened to the line by two or three twists around the central column and over the centre lug. This simple attachment means that they can be raised or lowered with ease to any depth, and that more than the normal two or three booms can be attached. But there is a disadvantage with French booms in that a heavy fish will slide them down the line, which leads to some stretching and distortion if monofilament is used. This can also weaken the line.

A single-trace boom can be used either as a running or a fixed ledger and is especially useful if a long trace is to be allowed to flow with the tide. In its fixed state it will allow several feet of monofilament to lie away from the line without tangling. But it has a specific use over rocky ground in its running form, used with a length of low b.s. line with which to attach the weight. Should a snag occur, then the finer line will part, allowing the main tackle to be retrieved. The wide angle between the points of the boom helps to keep both bait and trace from tangling around the main line.

There are several booms specially for ledgering, the best known being the Kilmore boom. In its simple form this consists of a loop of wire leading to a swivel and lead attachment. The loop through which the line is passed can be plain, or fitted with an inner ring of porcelain, or harder-wearing metal. The latter are the better choice, for plain wire in constant use causes line damage. If the porcelain-lined model is used, take care to mount a bead stop between the eye and trace swivel, otherwise a hard knock will cause the brittle lining to fracture. A major disadvantage of the Kilmore boom is that the lead hangs from the bottom of the boom, causing the trace which hangs past it to tangle, either when the rig is descending to the bottom, or between rebaiting and casting, when the lead naturally swings freely.

The Clements boom

The Clements boom is designed to prevent such tangling. The wire boom has a large eye twisted in either end, and from the end of one of these loops hangs the lead attachment. The reel line is threaded through the loops so that the lead attachment hangs farthest away from the trace. This gives a cantilever effect to the boom, making it stand at right-angles to the line and holding the trace well away from the lead. Again, there are several different types of lining fitted into the eyes of the boom, but it pays to use one that will help to counteract wear.

A long trace with a Clements boom means that the stop would have to be fastened 8ft or so from the end hook, which could lead to problems when landing a fish. There is a release Clements boom on the market which has a small inner cylinder along the body, through which the line is passed. With the cylinder pressed against the line the boom will stop in place, but once reeled tightly against the rod tip, the cylinder will free itself, allowing the whole rig to slide down to the end of the trace. The fish can then be played to the surface and landed.

There are many other sea rigs available, and it interesting to note that in many of them, plastic is now being used as the principal material. But most of the new arrivals are merely variations on the basic themes described above.

The single-eyed Kilmore boom, and variants on the double-eyed Clements boom, designed to prevent line and trace from tangling.

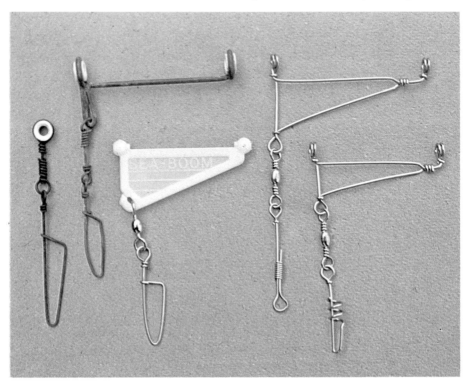

Sea fishing clothing

Sea fishing is a rugged, all-the-year-round sport. It takes the keen angler out in weather of every kind, and in order to enjoy it to the full he needs to have enough of the right kind of clothing to match the varied conditions he is likely to encounter.

Summer conditions

For warm, fairly windless weather, jeans and an old shirt are basic attire. Over the top, to provide extra warmth and to keep other clothing clean, a Cornish-style fisherman's smock can be worn, a bib-and-brace or zip-fronted overall, or a windproof anorak.

Following a hot afternoon it can suddenly turn very chilly, so a thick polo-neck sweater should be carried, and a set of lightweight PVC nylon waterproofs—a jacket with attached hood and high waisted bib trousers.

While non-slip deck shoes are excellent for boat fishing, strong leather boots (well waterproofed with dubbin) will be found more comfortable for walking the beach— particularly over difficult terrains like soft shingle, pebbles, boulders and rocks. Boots with cleated rubber soles provide a firm footing on clean rock, but extra grip is needed when negotiating surfaces covered with wet, slippery weed. An important aid in such conditions is a set of strap-on ABU rock-fishing spikes, which cut through the weed and hold tight on the solid rock beneath. Studded boots (golf studs are first class) are safest over needle grass and clay sediments.

For fishing at night there is nothing more comfortable than a one-piece waterproof suit with attached hood, stormproof thigh pockets, and elasticated wrists and ankles. The most expensive versions are thickly padded, and splendid to lie down on when resting during beach fishing.

Winter conditions

A padded fishing suit is quite warm enough without a lot of additional clothing underneath, but an unlined suit or an ordinary

Irish Tourist Board

Tackling up while the boat heads for the mark. Keep fishing and other gear tidy. Extra clothing should be kept dry in the cabin, but ready for use.

jacket-and-overtrousers set must be combined with proper undergarments to fully keep out the cold.

A mistake often made when dressing for cold weather is to smother the skin with tight-fitting clothing. This prevents air from circulating round the body, and once stale, air drops in temperature. Shirts and sweaters must be reasonably loose fitting for maximum comfort.

String or open-mesh underwear is first-class for cold-weather fishing, as are pyjamas and even ladies' tights. But by far the finest is

Sea fishing clothing

(Below) Lifejackets must all conform to British Standards specification BS 3595. The angler is also wearing good shoes for boat fishing and waterproofs. (Below, right) When fishing from the beach you must keep feet warm and dry. The one-piece suit is ideal.

Ken Whitehead

a one-piece Long John underwear suit specifically designed to combat sub-zero temperatures. A garment of this type has the ability to retain and reflect back the body's natural warmth, and worn beneath thick clothing will give ample protection in the severest of conditions.

Traditional seaboot stockings, or several pairs of thin socks, are adequate undercover for the feet on most days. But at night and for freezing days, bootliners are vastly superior for the greatly increased warmth they generate. Rubber-cleated leather boots, or rubber boots are suitable for boat fishing, and waders for shore fishing.

If a hat is worn at sea it must fit snugly, or else a sudden gust will be sure to blow it over the side. It is a good idea to sew one end of a

length of tape to the hat, and attach the other end to the jacket collar.

Of the many kinds of suitable headgear available, knitted hats are very popular, as are fur-lined, peaked, waterproof caps, with pull-down ear flaps that secure under the chin. A scarf or towel should be worn round the neck.

Hands are the most difficult part of the body to keep warm. Here there is no complete answer to this problem: only aids which reduce the discomfort to some extent. If it is necessary to hold the rod all the time, a pair of fingerless gloves will give a certain amount of protection. Woollen gloves, however, are not much good, as they soon become wet through. The only really sensible choice is a pair of fleece-lined leather gloves waterproofed against all the usual causes of wetness, with fairly long wrists so that they can be tucked up into the jacket sleeves.

If the rod is placed on a rest between bites, the hands, in addition to fingerless gloves, can be kept warm inside fur-lined mittens hung on a cord placed round the neck. Over-gloves must be spacious enough to allow for quick withdrawal of the hands.

Dressed in the cold-weather clothing

Irish Tourist Board

described so far, warmth depends solely on naturally generated heat being trapped and reflected back to the body by the structure and thickness of the layers. One disadvantage of this process is that it saps a great deal of energy. Another is that the angler, clad in such bulky gear, has less freedom of movement for casting and playing fish.

Waterproof boots and waders

Knee boots and thigh waders are standard equipment for sea angling. Shore fishermen also find chest waders very helpful at times; for example, when wading for bass along an Atlantic storm beach.

Boots and waders are made from plastic as well as rubber. Plastic types are lighter, more flexible, and allow the feet to breathe, which increases warmth. They are also more

hygienic having no lining and can be washed and dried regularly and easily.

Boots and waders should be kept in a cool corner away from direct light to prevent deterioration. Waders should be hung upside down on wader-clips, rather than left folded over, as they soon weaken along folds causing them to leak.

The irritating problem of socks rubbing inside boots and waders—gradually being pulled down over the ankles and off the feet—can be dealt with by wearing heel grips. Heel grips hold socks firmly in place against the heel by means of elasticated straps across the front of the feet. Boot and waders intended for use with thick socks or bootliners must be bought at least one size larger than normal foot size.

Camouflage

Although sea anglers favour brightly coloured red, orange and yellow outergarments, situations do occur that require drab clothing. Stalking big harbour mullet is a classic example of such a need. It takes a carefully concealed approach and a well presented bait to tempt mullet browsing in clear water, and the angler, to stand a good chance of being successful, needs clothing which camouflages with his background.

Dark clothing is usually the answer, but when it is necessary to angle from a position directly above the fish—from a jetty, for example—it is advantageous to dress in pale clothing, to blend with the sky rather than the harbour surroundings.

Final points

Clothing smeared with bait and fish slime will take on a strong and extremely repulsive smell if it is left uncleaned for any length of time. Waterproofs should be thoroughly sponged down with warm, fresh water, after each trip, and soiled clothing put to soak without delay.

It is never advisable to wear studded boots for boat fishing. Apart from the fact that they are dangerously slippery on deck boards, they scratch protective varnish and damage woodwork. Most skippers do not allow anglers to go aboard wearing them.

Lugworm

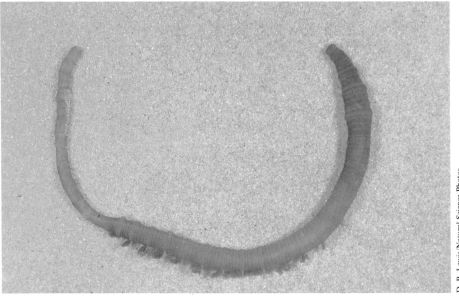

The lugworm, *Arenicola marina*, is one of the most popular of all baits used in sea angling, particularly with anglers fishing the East Anglian and Kent coasts. It is a smaller species than that other very popular choice of sea anglers, the King Ragworm, but when used from beach or boat it can be one of the deadliest baits for cod.

Ninety per cent of the sea fish found around the British Isles will usually take this bait readily, and besides being ideal for cod, it is particularly useful for the smaller varieties of flatfish – plaice, dabs and flounders. Many inland sea anglers prefer to buy a day's supply of lugworm from their local tackle shop, but anybody can dig an adequate supply for himself.

The best environment

The lugworm prefers sheltered beaches with a good depth of top sand and where the sea has a low salinity. River estuaries, therefore, provide the best environment. One never has to travel far along the British coastline to encounter such habitats –

Whitstable, Dale Fort, St Andrews, Millport, the south coast of the Isle of Man, Clew Bay on the West Coast of Ireland, are just a few of the many well-known areas where the lugworm can be dug in numbers. Size and colouring can vary considerably from area to area – in some cases there is a marked difference between the worms dug from the same sandy bay – due to environmental factors.

The common lugworm is often known as the 'blow' lug to differentiate it from the black lug which is very thick-skinned and requires gutting to prolong the time it will keep, and from the Deal yellow-tail, a worm peculiar to the south side of the Stour Estuary in Kent.

Lugworm live in a U-shaped burrow in the sand, the entrances of which are marked at one end by the tell-tale spiral casts and at the other by a depression in the sand known as the blow hole, through which the worm draws its food. Into the tunnel fall particles of sand mixed with water and organic matter, all of which the worm eats. The organic matter is digested and the sand is excreted, forming the cast at the other end of the burrow.

For digging the common lugworm the ordinary flat-tined potato fork is the best tool; a spade chops too many worms in half. Lugworm casts are found on any sandy beach below high water mark but, normally, the nearer to the extreme low water mark the greater the number of casts to be found and the bigger the worms. If the sand is covered in casts no more than 2 or 3in apart, then worms can be dug by trenching, that is, digging the sand as one would the garden. However, if signs are few and far between, 'singling' is best. This involves removing the sand between the blow hole and the cast, thus uncovering the worm after about three forkfuls. The burrow is lined with mucus from the worm's body, giving it a bright orange colour rather like rust, and enabling the angler to see exactly which way the burrow is running at each forkful.

(Above left) The lugworm, showing the gill fronds in the centre part of the body, and the hard bristles, or chaetae.
(Below) The asymmetrical casts of the common lugworm, different from the spiral-coil casts of the Deal yellow-tail.

The worms should be removed to a clean wooden box or plastic bucket. Never use a galvanized pail as the zinc kills the worm very quickly. When sufficient worms have been dug, they should be washed in clean sea water to remove all particles of sand as well as any worms pierced by the fork. These should be put into a separate container for, although they will live as long as the whole worms, the blood exuded by their wounds has an adverse effect on the others.

Storing lugworm

When you return home, the worms should be placed on clean, dry newspaper in a single layer, with another piece laid on top so that the bait is sandwiched between two sheets of paper. If the weather is cold, the temperature not rising above 4.4°C (40°F), and the worms are stored in a garage or outhouse, they will stay in good condition for 4-5 days. In the summer, when temperatures are high, this life is reduced to less than 36 hours unless the worms are refrigerated. Another method of keeping worms alive until required is to place them in a well-aerated saltwater-filled aquarium. With this method care must be taken to remove any dead worms immediately, before they can pollute the water.

Unfortunately, the peak of autumn cod fishing coincides with the time when lugworm is most difficult to obtain, for it is spawning. Although the actual day it occurs varies from colony to colony, in nearly all areas spawning takes place between the last week of September and the middle of November. Lugworms are not hermaphrodite (having characteristics of both sexes) but sexed male and female. The eggs of the females and the sperms of the males begin to accumulate from mid-summer onwards, moving around in the body fluid and giving the worms a milky appearance. If a worm is broken this fluid will be found to be rather sticky and slimy.

When the worms are ripe, the spawn of both sexes is released onto the sand, where fertilization occurs. If the worm survives the spawning it will go right to the bottom of its burrow and remain immobile for two or

G. E. Hyde

Lugworm

Digging for lug. Tedious but necessary when bait costs are considered.

three weeks while it recovers. During this period it eats very little, creating no tell-tale casts to mark its presence, so that sands that previously appeared to contain millions of worms, now seem completely barren.

Four or five days after spawning, the larva hatches. About 1/100in long, it is pear-shaped, opaque, and bears no resemblance to the adult worm. By early spring it has taken the form of the adult and is found high in the sand, working its way downwards as it matures. At two years old it spawns for the first time and usually lives to spawn a second time, at three years, this time the lug dies.

The Deal yellow-tail

There is evidence that adult lugworm will come out of the sand and swim freely in the sea. This phenomenon usually occurs in the early spring. The Deal yellow-tail is probably a sub-species of *Arenicola marina,* although many authorities believe it to appear different simply through environmental factors. However, the worm behaves entirely differently from the common lugworm. The cast, instead of being a haphazard spiral, is perfectly symmetrical, and the worm burrows to a greater depth than the common lug.

The yellow-tail is generally larger, and when dug appears very limp, seeming, to the uninitiated, to be dead. It also has the peculiar habit of coiling itself into a circle when held in the palm of the hand, whereas the common lug will only bend slightly. The best way of keeping the yellow-tail – its name derives from the bright yellow stain it leaves on the hands – is in clean sea water.

Another sub-species is the black lug, which is even bigger than the Deal yellow-tail and has a very thick skin. It often lives in a mixture of mud and sand, where the most successful way of obtaining it is to use a small, long-handled spade, digging straight down from the cast and following the trail until the worm is sighted. It is rarely possible to trench for this worm.

Roll them in newspaper

Immediately after digging, the intestines and blood should be squeezed out through the head end and, to keep them in perfect condition, the worms should be rolled singly in sheets of newspaper. The black lug is large enough to provide several small baits from a single worm, although for cod fishing a whole worm should be threaded on the hook. Because it is tough, it makes an ideal bait for beachcasting.

Common lug can be threaded either singly or doubly, depending on size, when beach fishing for cod, but for boat fishing it is usually better to hang them from the bend of the hook, just passing the hook in and out of the body where the sandy tail section joins the fat part. The number of worms put on a hook depends, first, on the size of the worm and, second, on the size of the fish expected. When fishing for varieties of small flatfish, a largish worm may be broken in half to provide ample bait for a small mouth.

Ragworm

Just as the soil of the countryside is a home for many kinds of earthworm, so the seabed provides sanctuary for many kinds of marine worm. One of the commonest species is the ragworm, of which several kinds exist.

The ragworm differs from the lugworm in that it tapers very gradually from head to tail and is much fleshier. Most ragworms are bright red and all varieties have hundreds of 'legs' down each side of the body. The head is armed with a pair of bony pincers which the worm can thrust out and retract at will and a large worm can inflict a painful bite on the unwary angler.

Where the ragworm is found

King ragworm is probably the most common and the most sought-after for bait. The angler can obtain two large, or several smaller baits, from a good-sized specimen which can be over 2ft long. The worm is found close to the high-water mark but the nearer one goes to the low-water spring-tide mark, the more prolific it becomes—although this varies from coast to coast as does the worm itself. The best localities are estuaries where there is a mixture of river mud and shell, where it lives in a U-shaped burrow, the sides cemented with mucus from its body. Once it has dug its home the worm can propel itself through the tunnel with its many 'legs'. The bait-digger seeking this worm treads the ground carefully, watching for a water-spout pushed up when the burrow is compressed by his boot. If worms are scarce it pays to locate both entrances to the tunnel and remove the soil between, looking for the tell-tale burrow. In some areas you may have to dig to a depth of 2ft or more to secure the worm. Where there is an abundance of worms, and each footfall produces several jets of water, 'trenching' is the best method. A good day's supply of bait can be obtained from one hole.

At spawning-time the king ragworm changes its bright red colour (with a pale green back) into a slate green and, when broken, exudes a slimy, milky liquid. During this season, which varies from area to area but is usually in spring, the worm is of very little use as bait. One interesting fact, however, is that during the breeding season, large numbers of worms leave the safety of their burrows and swim freely in the sea. If, as often happens, there is a sudden on-shore wind, great numbers are thrown up by the breakers onto the beach, either to die in the sun, or be swallowed by seagulls.

All worms deteriorate very quickly in high temperatures and, once dug, they should be dried and cooled as soon as possible. Whole, undamaged worms should be wrapped singly in newspaper and stored at 2°C in a refrigerator, where they can be kept in good condition for more than a week. Damaged worms should be separated and used first.

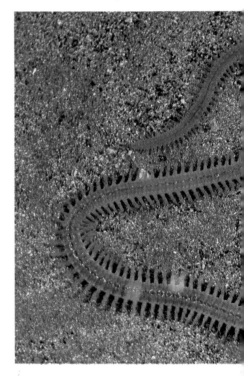

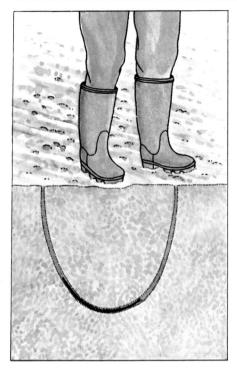

Rod Sutterby

D. B. Lewis/Natural Science Photos

(Above) The ragworm's mucus-lined burrow.
(Left) The ragworm, Nereis (Neanthes)
virens, *strikingly coloured.*

But if keeping is not important—perhaps all
the worms are going to be used next day—
they will keep perfectly in a box of
vermiculite (insulating granules).

Mounting the bait

King ragworm can be an extremely
effective bait, particularly for bass and
pollack. For these fighting predators, worms
up to 1ft long can be used whole. Secure just
the head on the hook, leaving the rest
trailing. Mounted in this way it is very lifelike and pollack and bass rarely bite short.
They have insatiable appetites and take the
whole worm into their mouth before making
off with it. The largest worms can be cut in
half and baited in a similar way. Other
species that prefer ragworm to lugworm are
flounder, thornback ray, dogfish and
smooth-hound.

White ragworm is a variety which has

become very popular over the past few years, particularly with beach anglers. It is smaller than the king ragworm, one 8in long being a good specimen. Because it is a very localized worm it cannot be dug in sufficient numbers to ensure regular commercial supplies.

The white ragworm lives in sheltered bays where there is an abundance of soft yellow sand, although it is sometimes found in the same area as king ragworm if there is fine surface gravel. A relatively shallow-burrowing worm, the white ragworm is rarely found more than 9in deep, and often only 2in or 3in, below the surface. Because it gives no indication of its whereabouts, digging must be 'hit or miss', the search limited only by choosing the right kind of ground. No visible change occurs in the white ragworm during the breeding period but, like other varieties in the species, it comes up from the sand and swims freely in the sea.

Preserving the white ragworm

The white ragworm does not keep as well as the king ragworm and the most useful preservative is a plastic bucket full of fresh seawater. As well as being much smaller than its cousin the king ragworm, the white ragworm is also more delicate, and a fine gauge wire hook is recommended to avoid damaging the worm.

Rockies are another small member of the family and, as the name implies, they are found in chalk rocks among deposits of mud and sand in sheltered bays. These deposits tend to fill the natural crevices in the chalk outcrops and the worm lives in these, so that a pick-axe is more useful than a fork for prizing this bait from its habitat.

Rockies and Maddies

Rarely exceeding 5in or 6in, the rocky is a very active worm with bright red colouring. To keep it at its best, put it into a box of fine grit dampened with seawater. In a refrigerator it should remain active for three or four days. As with the white rag, a fine wire hook is recommended to avoid undue damage when baiting. Presented in this way white ragworm will catch the same species of fish as the king ragworm.

Maddies are the smallest member of the family, rarely growing to more than 3in in length. They are most likely to be found in estuary and harbour mud, living like the king ragworm in burrows lined with the mucus from their bodies. Because the mud is smooth, the tunnel entrances appear as large pin-pricks on the surface. When the area is trodden upon the tiny holes emit small spouts of water. Maddies appear to live in colonies for it is not unusual to dig as many as 30 worms with one forkful. Its small size and soft environment make it a delicate worm and one very difficult to keep alive for more than 24 hours. It is highly esteemed as bait for mullet fishing, particularly in and around harbours and, fished on a small hook it is an excellent bait for garfish.

Hooking a Ragworm

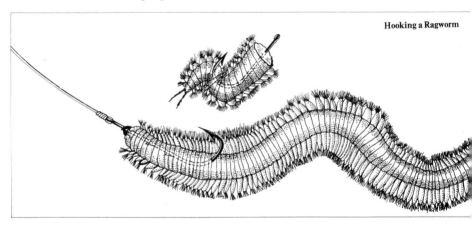

Ken Whitehead

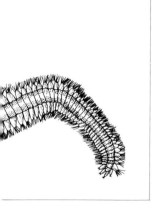

Lyn Cawley

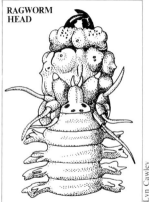

RAGWORM HEAD

(Above) Differently coloured from the specimen shown on the previous pages, but still the familiar king ragworm, Nereis virens.

(Far left) Two ways to put ragworm on the hook.

(Left) Top, or dorsal view of the head of the king ragworm in its protruded form. The eyes can be seen as four dots just before the body segments begin.

Mackerel

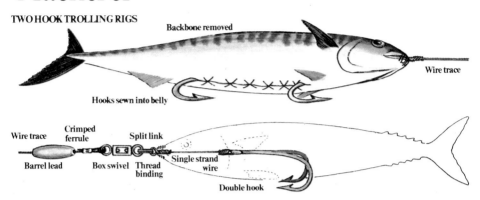

Backbone removed

Wire trace

Hooks sewn into belly

Wire trace · Crimped ferrule · Split link

Barrel lead · Box swivel · Thread binding · Single strand wire

Double hook

Of all the fish species inhabiting Britain's coastal waters, there is none with a more mixed reputation than that enjoyed by the mackerel. Although some rate them highly for a variety of reasons, there are those who dismiss them as 'dirty eaters', or as being too easy to catch or not worth eating. But as a fish bait, a fresh mackerel has no equal.

What makes the fish so attractive as a bait? In short, it is the mackerel's abundant body juices, rich in oils and vitamins, a characteristic shared with the herring and salmon. Fish are able to detect these juices by the sense of smell which all species, to a greater or lesser degree, possess. Because of its attraction, it is important that mackerel is used only when in prime condition.

Feathering

Mackerel may be taken in various ways, although the majority are caught by boat anglers using sets of hooks dressed with feathers. 'Feathering' is a good method, as up to six hooks can be used and, on occasions, a greedy mackerel will be caught on each, thus providing a plentiful supply of bait. Some fishermen advocate other methods, such as highly efficient sets of Norwegian lures, in which metal alternatives with rubber tubing cut to imitate the eel.

No matter how efficient the lure may be, however, it will not produce results if fished at the wrong depth. It is important to

(Above) Two trolling rigs, one using a double hook, the other with singles in tandem. (Right) The attraction of mackerel lies in its rich and oily flesh. (Below) Injecting a mackerel head with pilchard oil as an added attraction for conger. (Far right) A mackerel tail fished on a running ledger with a wire trace is one of the standard methods used by anglers concentrating on conger.

remember that the mackerel, not possessing a swim bladder, can move surprisingly fast and so a shoal can change depth very rapidly. If several anglers are on board it is advisable for them to fish at different depths until a shoal is located. When very calm conditions prevail, as is often the case at first light, watch for sudden turbulence on an empty patch of sea—this could well be caused by mackerel just below the surface.

Mackerel as bait can be fished in a variety of ways, and methods of presentation attractive to most species can be found. Two important considerations must be borne in mind, whatever style of fishing is to be employed. First, the bait size and pre-sentation should be appropriate to the quarry and its manner of feeding; secondly, the bait and hook should be matched in size.

Apart from its other advantages, the mackerel's shape and bone structure make it an ideal bait form. It can be cut in different ways according to requirements. The section adjoining the caudal or tail fin provides on each side a near-triangular patch known as a 'lask' or 'last'. This is recommended for bream, whiting, and other small species. Remember, though, that while various species may be of roughly similar size, their mouths are quite dissimilar—a fact to be considered when selecting hooks and cutting bait to match. An over-large bait can mask the barb so that hooking the fish becomes virtually impossible.

Alternatively, a side or flank can be offered, either whole, halved or sliced into strips to resemble small fish. To hook a half-side or strip of mackerel, drive the hook right through the fish and then twist this to allow

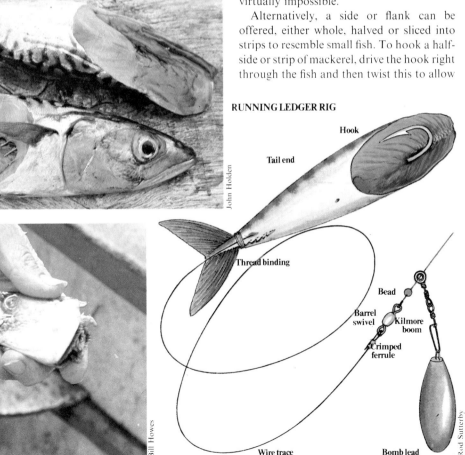

RUNNING LEDGER RIG

Hook

Tail end

John Holden

Thread binding

Bead

Barrel swivel

Kilmore boom

Crimped ferrule

Bill Howes

Wire trace

Bomb lead

Rod Sutterby

the hook to come through again in a different place. This ensures that maximum benefit is gained from the oily flesh.

A whole side of mackerel can be held in position and presented in an attractive manner by whipping a small hook onto the trace a couple of inches above the main hook. The top of the bait is then supported, the lower portion being free to move with the current to simulate a small live fish.

A mackerel sliced diagonally across its body from just below the gill cover on one side to a point near the vent on the other, makes an ideal top bait, as indeed does the head complete with entrails. To obtain the latter, the fish should be cut around the 'shoulders' so that the head comes free with the innards attached. Here again, the important thing is to exploit the fish-attracting juices. This bait is excellent when float-fished. To secure it, pass the hook through the head adjacent to the eye.

Conger can often be lured by a whole mackerel. Use a baiting needle to draw the

(Above) For large fish such as cod, needing large hooks, a whole side of fresh mackerel is ideal. Thread the hook through. (Above, right) A side of mackerel cut into strips will bait a dozen hooks.

(Below) Fresh mackerel on a running ledger. Note the breakaway casting lead.

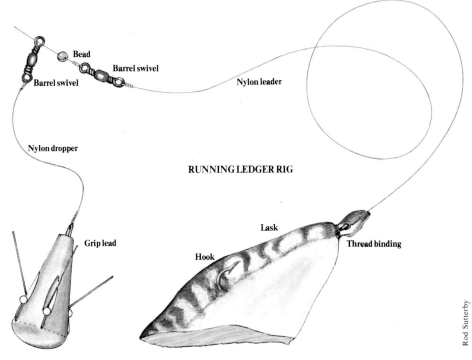

RUNNING LEDGER RIG

Bead

Barrel swivel

Barrel swivel

Nylon leader

Nylon dropper

Grip lead

Lask

Hook

Thread binding

Rod Sutterby

John Holden

hook into position. Some anglers draw the hook up to the vent, others prefer it to protrude from the bait's flank. Whichever method is used, slash the skin in several places to release the blood and oily juices.

When using large baits of this kind, the tide's motion will frequently cause them to spin and so impart an amount of twist to the trace. To overcome this, use at least one, swivel between the reel line and hook.

For most sea anglers the mackerel is a summer species. This leads to an obvious question: what does one use when fresh mackerel are not available as bait? In some areas, the South West for example, mackerel are caught professionally throughout the winter, weather permitting, and can be bought fresh from fishmongers. In other regions, though, when the fish have travelled to inland fishmongers via the wholesale market, and then, after being bought as bait by the angler, they can be very wrinkled, unattractive specimens.

For anglers with a deep-freeze, a great saving can be made by catching early morning mackerel and then freezing them for later use. But fish which have been dead for hours, and lying in the sun in an open boat, do not freeze properly for when unfrozen they will rapidly deteriorate into a soft and useless mass. At one time the alternative solution was simple—use her-

ring. This species was cheap and plentiful. They are still an excellent bait, but over-fishing has led to a scarcity and high prices.

Having dealt with the mackerel as a bait, let us return briefly to its defence in other spheres. The mackerel is not a 'dirty eater' but is a predator which chases and kills other fish, although there is a period during spring and early summer when plankton become its prime diet.

Competition for food

That mackerel can be easy to catch cannot be denied. This is certainly true of most, if not all, shoaling species. The competition for food can be so great that individuals will throw themselves on anything attractive, as witness the savagery with which a pack of spurdog will dispute possession of a bait, or the way whiting will snap at potential food. The larger the shoal the greater the competition, and nowadays there are few species to be found in greater abundance than mackerel.

A mackerel long-since caught and stale is a sad offering as a table fish. But one fresh from the sea is a real delight. Unfortunately, no fish becomes soft and unappetizing more rapidly, and so remember that mackerel caught on a summer's morn, subjected to the heat of the day and then taken, perhaps, on a long journey home, will be stale and far from the tasty dish they can be.

Squid and cuttlefish

The flesh of squid, cuttlefish and to a lesser extent octopus makes super bait to tempt many species of sea fish. They belong to the class Cephalopoda, and are cylinder or sac-shaped molluscs with suckered tentacles surrounding the mouth and joining the head. The eyes are conspicuous, and the mouth is equipped with horny jaws like a bird of prey's beak.

Squid have a 'quill' or backbone closely resembling plastic, while the shell of the cuttlefish is a familiar sight on beaches.

The squid is most commonly used as bait, as its distribution in the Atlantic, English

cleaned by severing the head and cutting evenly down through the centre of the body to the tail. It should then be opened and laid out flat, and the stomach removed in one easy movement. With care you can do this without bursting the ink sac which has an acid content irritating to human skin. Squid wings are useless as bait and can be thrown away. Finally, it needs thorough washing using two changes of fresh water, and then the bait is ready for freezing.

If you are preparing a number of squid at the same time, it is a good policy to pack them in polythene bags holding just enough

(Left) A large cuttlefish. (Below and right) Stages in the preparation of a squid for bait. Keep the head separate as conger bait.

P. H. Ward/Natural Science Photos

Channel and North Sea brings it within range of trawlers operating at ports dotted around the coastline. Cuttlefish are frequently caught but in nothing like the numbers of squid. The octopus is a rare catch in British waters, but a few are hooked by anglers fishing on very rough ground for more conventional species.

Advantages of squid bait

Squid is the cleanest bait to use in sea fishing as the flesh is firm, cuts cleanly and easily, and can be presented attractively in a variety of ways. Above all it keeps well, and a supply laid down in a freezer can stay perfectly fresh for two years. This applies if you follow simple rules. The squid must be thoroughly

for a day's fishing. Failure to do this will almost certainly result in wasted bait, as once thawed out it cannot be refrozen.

Freeze the heads separately

Squid heads make a great bait for conger, ling or any other large species, and should be frozen separately. If they are mixed in with the bodies of the squid and taken out on shore trips when small fry are the quarry, it is likely that only the tentacles will be used, which is wasteful.

Take a word of warning however. The freezing compartment of a domestic refrigerator is only suitable for keeping small quantities of squid for short periods.

If you do keep it there, make sure the lady

Rod Sutterby

'MURDERER'

Squid are rarely caught on rod and line, but they can be taken with a 'murderer'. It is used like a pirk or jig.

of the house knows about it. Disasters can occur when a refrigerator is switched off for de-frosting, and the squid is left in the top.

Squid caught on rod and line

Although most squid are obtained from commercial sources, they can be caught fairly easily on rod and line during the winter months when they shoal in vast numbers particularly at the western end of the English Channel. Between October and March they can be a problem in deep water as they snatch at baits put out for pollack and coalfish with a 'take' that is similar to those of both species. The similarity ends after the take however, as they let the bait go a few feet from the boat, even after making a number of powerful dives giving the impression that they are securely hooked.

For a reason that has never been clear, the squid is seldom caught on normal tackle. It is

10 fathoms deep. The average weight is 2-3lb, but specimens to 10lb are not uncommon. In fact, it is generally the larger squid that are caught on rod and line.

All fish will take squid, and some species particularly relish it. Heading the list are red and black bream, which are caught in their thousands on very thin strips about 3in long offered on fine hooks to paternosters, or a single hook on a flowing trace.

Change a frayed bait

As the squid is so tough, it is possible to catch several bream on the same strip of bait. As soon as the edges show signs of fraying however, it must be changed. Hundreds of conger eels to 100lb are also taken on squid head, or a whole squid hooked through the body and ledgered close to a wreck or on rough ground. Similarly it is a great favourite with the ravenous ling.

Mike Millman

a crafty fish. To outwit them, the angler uses a murderer—a weighted body about 4in long fitted with two rings of needle-sharp points at one end of the lure. Jigged about 10ft below the surface, it will hook any squid that strikes at it on one of the many points. When the catch is lifted over the side, watch out for the ink which the squid will pump out.

The squid cannot be used as bait immediately after capture as the flesh is jelly-like and almost transparent, to the extent that you can see its vital organs. Six hours after death the flesh changes to the familiar white rubbery texture.

Most rod-caught squid are taken within a few feet of the surface, but in water less than

A strip of squid about 10in long and 1in wide cut to resemble a fish, makes a fine trolling bait for bass. Mounted on a long-shanked hook and worked astern at about three knots, it will dart about in a realistic manner and soon find a taker.

For shore fishing on storm beaches, squid is ideal bait as it stands up to long casting and can take any amount of battering from heavy surf. Many flatfish enthusiasts use it extensively as a bottom bait for turbot, plaice and dabs, although it has never been much good for flounder.

During the winter months, monster mackerel have a definite liking for a thin strip of squid, and give great sport on light tackle.

Sandeel

The sandeel is not only one of the best baits for sea angling, but a very important part of the food chain for most species of fish. Three varieties are found in British waters: the greater sandeel *(Hyperoplus lanceolatus)* which can be easily identified by the black spot on the sides of the snout, the sandeel *(Ammodytes tobianus)* and the smooth sandeel *(Gymnammodytes semisquamatus)*.

They have elongated bodies and no spiny rays in the fins. The upper jaw is extensible and shorter than the lower, and the tail fin is forked and separate from the dorsal and anal.

When and where to find sandeel

Sandeels shoal in very large numbers but are seldom seen in daylight as they lie buried in the sand. They emerge after dark, and the light from a torch will often reveal what appears to be a solid shimmering mass in the shallow water of sandy estuaries. Sandeels are generally caught by towing a fine-mesh seine net from a small rowing boat off sandy beaches, or by digging and raking in the sand on the beach. The latter is best done at low tide right at the water's edge, as the eels like to hide in very wet sand. If there is a freshwater stream running down the beach this is also a good place to search.

The speedy sandeel

Most sandeels are dug for at night when it is customary to work by the light of a pressure lamp. Once an eel has been lifted out of the sand it must be picked up immediately as it has the ability to tunnel back extremely quickly. In fact, a 7in eel, when placed on very firm sand, can disappear beneath the surface in less than two seconds.

Collecting by hand will produce about 30 eels in a couple of hours—more than enough

Mike Millman

(Above) To keep sandeels alive it is necessary to use a portable pump to aerate the water. The fish need a high level of oxygen to remain alive.
(Below left) Sandeels and artificials.

bait for a day's fishing. A seine net, however, will trap as many as 10,000 eels in a single run of less than half an hour. The net is weighted at the bottom with rolling leads and supported by cork floats which keep it upright and level with the surface. It is paid out from the stern of a rowing boat which slowly describes a circle about 50 yards out from the beach. One end of the holding rope is kept onshore by a member of the three-man team, and when the net has been completely laid, the other end is brought ashore. The seine is then pulled smoothly in until the bag is clear of the water.

During sorting, a careful watch should be kept for poisonous weever-fish, which are frequently caught during sandeel operations. Eels over 5in are retained and the rest quickly returned to the sea.

Keeping sandeels alive during transportation was a problem until quite recently. Sandeels depend on a high level of oxygen in water and, if this falls below a certain level, they die within a few minutes. Fortunately,

small, battery-operated air-pumps are now on the market, and can run as long as 30 hours on a couple of 1.5-volt dry cell batteries.

A reliable aerator
The Shakespeare company produces a reliable pump which is light and compact and currently retails at £5.96. A matching heavy duty PVC livebait-carrying bag currently costs £2.33. The bag, which holds a gallon of water and becomes rigid when full, is perfect for keeping bait in good condition. It also features a water level gauge that indicates the maximum volume of water that can be aerated by this motor-pump. In many ways this outfit is one of the best contributions to angling for many years.

As sandeels are plentiful in the summer but extremely scarce after October, livebaiting during the dark months will necessitate keeping a stock of sandeels at home. All you need is a large glass tank of the type sold by shops catering for tropical fish enthusiasts, a couple of filter boards, and a mains air pump. A tank 3ft long by 1ft wide and 18in deep holds enough water to keep 200 eels alive for a long period. The bottom of the tank should be covered by 8in of sand for the eels to bury in, and it is advisable to remove 10 gallons of water every so often and replace it with a new supply of seawater. Sandeels do not require feeding as they filter plankton from the water and find other forms of marine life in the sand. To supplement their feeding, add a few large pieces of seaweed to the tank from time to time.

The courge
Before the introduction of air pumps, the angler had to use a floating courge to keep sandeels alive. For hundreds of years they were made professionally from wickerwork in a variety of sizes, but the trade died out in the 1920s. They were pointed at both ends with a trap door in the top and could be towed behind a sailing or rowing boat so the eels were maintained in an almost natural environment. The modern equivalent is a wooden box, with one pointed end and many small holes, which allow the passage of

Mike Millman

water. It can be towed behind a slow craft without damaging the eels, but is usually placed in the water on a tether, when the boat is either drifting or at anchor over a mark.

During the journey out, the eels are kept fresh in a plastic drum to which buckets of seawater are constantly added. Some boats with glass-fibre hulls have livebait tanks built in at the water-line. A constant change of water can be obtained by simply opening a sea-cock. With this refinement, both eels and other fish can be kept alive indefinitely.

Catching sandeels

During boat fishing trips in deep water, sandeels are occasionally caught by accident on feathers intended for mackerel. To fish for them selectively, however, you need to be over sandy banks where there is a fast run of tide. Such a place is the Skerries Bank off the Devon coast, renowned for its turbot, plaice and dab fishing. Between the Skerries Buoy at the eastern end and Start Point at the west, the banks are covered by varying depths of water. Sandeels swarm in millions here, and

(Above) A wooden courge. Attached to the boat and left floating, the holes allow seawater to pass through and keep the sandeels alive and fresh.
(Above right) Old-fashioned wicker courges, once universal, are now being replaced by the holed wooden boxes.
(Right) Two methods of baiting sandeel.

if you drop a set of feathers half a dozen times, you will collect enough for a good day's sport.

Many sandeels to 1ft in length are foul-hooked, but are considered too big for live use. Instead, thin even strips cut from just behind the head to the tail are used. When livebaiting, most expert sea anglers prefer eels with a light brown back, as these are livelier than those sporting a dark green hue.

To bait a sandeel, hold it firmly but lightly between the fingers and thumb, throat outwards. Put the point of the hook through the bottom lip and nick it into the soft skin of the belly just behind the head—this is the

Bill Howes

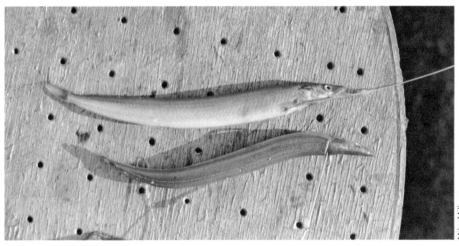

Mike Millman

normal way of offering it in a fair run of tide. When fishing in slack water, however, it is often better to simply hook the eel through the top of its body, in front of the dorsal.

Hooks for sandeels

Hooks must be long in the shank, needle-sharp, and fine in the wire—a description that fits the Aberdeen perfectly. Live eels must be offered on a very long trace, which allows them to swim around in a natural manner. The movement is enhanced if nylon monofilament with a b.s. of no more than 12lb is used.

Trolling with live or dead sandeels over rocky ground can be a rewarding business,

and big catches of pollack and bass are made. Of the many species partial to sandeel these two predators head the list, and even medium-weight fish of these species completely engulf a fair-sized eel in a single attack.

For shore fishing from rocky stations the live eel is best used with float gear, but the float should be sufficiently large to withstand the eel's thrashing without going under.

The eels can also be offered successfully as a spinning bait if you are fishing deep water from rocky ledges. This is general practice on the north coast of Cornwall, where the main quarry is bass, pollack and mackerel.

Rubber eels and lures

Mike Millman

For more than a hundred years, rod and line fishermen have used artificial lures to catch sea fish. Long before the start of this century, ingenious minds dreamed up many different types of baits that twisted, wobbled or travelled through the water with an undulating motion. The earliest lure was made from a length of wide rubber-band, one end whipped to the hook shank. It bore a remarkable resemblance to a living worm.

Sophisticated lures appear

From this beginning, more sophisticated lures soon evolved. Two types in particular, known as Brook's Double Twist Spinning Eel, and Captain Tom's Spinning Eel, were the first to be made from lengths of india-rubber pipe. This was pushed onto a large hook to form an 'elbow' at the bend, which caused it to spin when worked through the water at speed. Small brass swivels attached to the hook eye prevented the line from twisting to any great extent, and the top end of the pipe was securely fastened to the shank with stout thread.

In 1948, rubber gave way to plastic and the first modern eels appeared. The

A selection of modern, colourful lures for sea fishing. Their success depends upon movement to attract fish.

'Mevagissey', produced by Alex Ingram, was made by a dip-coating process. Early models featured a long, soft, curved tail, which plugged into a hollow body. When viewed from above, the lure had a natural-looking action, but it tended to spin, which caused the reel line to twist. One day, watching a jet landing with its braking parachute extended, Alex noted that this chute oscillated, and he realized that if the action could be incorporated into a sandeeel, its movement would be much improved. Over a period of time, various prototypes were tried out in the rugged conditions of wreck and reef fishing at many sites in Britain, until the 172mm Red Gill lure finally emerged that was to revolutionize sea fishing.

In the late 1960s dip-coating gave way to injection moulding, and improved plastics produced a much better eel. Modern PVC resists ultra-violet radiation and the effects of saltwater, so that lures now have tremen-

94

Steve Bicknell

(Left) Three models in the well-known range of colourful Toby lures.
(Below) A group of lures which the bass angler uses to attract his particular prey.

Mike Millman

dous durability. A boat angler fishing off Falmouth, who kept careful records of each fish he caught, noted that 199 pollack fell to the same Red Gill lure. Gradually the range has grown, and the latest is the 210mm Thresher, designed for wreck fishing.

Eddystone artificials have certainly made their mark on the sea angling scene since their introduction in 1974. Less sophisticated, but with a devastating tail action, they are now in wide use, and account for large numbers of big fish. Some models designed for spinning have a metal head plugged into the conventional plastic tail. This enables the lure to be cast a considerable distance, without the need for a spiral lead on the trace. Eddystone trolling lures with exceptionally long and very thin tails are also used with great success by anglers seeking bass and pollack.

Movement—the secret of success

No matter how good the design of an artificial sandeel, its success is totally dependent on one thing—movement. All have a negligible action of their own, and only movement imparted by an angler gives a lure 'life'. Unfortunately, this is not always realised, and one sees artificial sandeels being used garnished with a strip of mackerel, squid or—incredibly—a natural sandeel. Anything on the lure's hook will completely ruin its action.

Soft plastic can easily become deformed, too, if not handled with a reasonable amount of care and it is therefore important not to crush eels into a tackle box.

Plastic lures are available in a wide range of colours, but divers tell us that below 30ft, even in clear water conditions, colour (as we know it) begins to disappear. At 100ft it has gone altogether. So what is the point in painting artificials so attractively—most are used in depths of 40 fathoms (240ft) to which no light penetrates. The clue is surely in the phrase 'Colour *as we know it*'. The human eye may perceive quite differently from the fish's eye.

During 1972, a year when many outstanding pollack and coalfish were caught in deep water, red lures accounted for the greatest number, including the present British record pollack of 25lb. Lures of other colours were being offered in an identical manner, but got a very poor response. Consequently, red lures were so much in demand that supplies

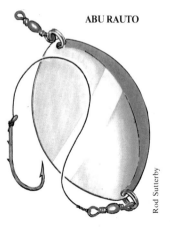

ABU RAUTO

Rod Sutterby

Bill Howes

ran out in the tackle shops, and stocks finished in green, yellow and blue were quickly given a coat of red paint.

Recent studies have shown that lures coloured deep purple with a blue head, and dark red with a gold belly are currently catching extremely well.

Profusion of metal lures

So far we have dealt only with plastic lures, but there are a great many manufactured in metal. This type is used extensively for shore spinning, and, to a lesser extent, trolling from small craft over inshore grounds. The range of shape and colour is bewildering. The newcomer to sea angling is easily confused by the profusion of different types, all of which profess to catch fish when, regrettably, most are designed to catch anglers. A recent estimate of the number of plastic, wood and metal lures originating in North America came to almost 4,000 kinds. While many are obviously the result of detailed study into the habits of certain species, the majority are completely worthless. It is a sad fact that many tackle shops in Britain now carry artificials that are equally ineffectual. Before parting with your money, therefore, take advice from anglers with experience in artificial lure fishing.

Spinning is now a very popular method with shore anglers. Development of suitable tackle has kept pace with the sport and hollow glass rods, fixed-spool and multiplier reels handle lures of $\frac{1}{8}$oz up to 4oz. All the beginner needs is a 7ft rod, a fixed-spool reel and 10lb b.s. line—£12 buys a good-quality outfit from a reputable manufacturer.

Among the most successful metal lures for spinning are Toby, Droppen, Spinflasha and Wingflasha, which have accounted for many fine bass, pollack, mackerel and garfish. In addition to the spoon used as a spinning bait, a spoon may also be used as an attractor for such species as bass, flounder and plaice. In this instance the fish is attracted by the spoon and takes the conventional bait. It is used by experts when working in estuaries and tidal rivers. Spoons take many forms—what is right in one place can be a complete flop in another. Many are home-made from brass, copper and occasionally plastic. Inventors pay great attention to the overall shape, thickness and twist of the blade, and to the colour, which many consider vital.

Swedish model

A commercially produced spoon that takes a lot of beating is ABU's Rauto. Among its captures in deeper water have been record cod on 6lb line, and much heavier fish on stronger tackle.

The search for new and better designs in both plastic and metal goes on. Many fish, especially bass, are becoming familiar with the appearance of current designs of plastic sandeels and show an added wariness, but there is little doubt that British manufacturers, who lead the world, intend to stay one jump ahead.

Peeler crabs

Many people believe, quite wrongly, that the peeler crab is not a crustacean, but, like all other crabs, it belongs to that group of creatures. These have their skeleton on the outside of their body and their muscles and organs inside it. Growth is only possible by changing shells, and this is done by growing a new, larger shell, which has at first to be soft in order to fit beneath the existing hard shell. When the new, soft shell is fully formed, just before the old one is discarded, the crab is known as a 'peeler'.

Common shore crab

Of the many varieties of crab found around our coasts, the best, and most widely used, for bait is the common shore crab *(Carcinus moenas)*. The young crab starts life from an egg which hatches in the upper layers of the sea. At this stage the larva bears no resemblance to the adult, but in a few weeks it undergoes five moults, after which it sinks to the seabed and takes on the characteristic form of a crab.

During the crab's early life moulting takes place frequently during the summer months, when the water is warm, but the process occurs less frequently in winter and as the crab matures. At the half-grown stage it will shed its shell twice or even three times a year, whereas the adult will change its shell very infrequently—probably every second year.

Immediately after casting off its shell the crab becomes what is known as a soft back or soft crab. At this stage it is defenceless and so hides itself, but a new shell begins to form straight away. After a few hours the shell is

In their peeler state crabs make a fine bait for many kinds of fish. A rocky coast has an endless supply of this bait.

Ken Whitehead

Peeler crabs

like parchment but the crab is still not at its best as a bait.

The colour of the common inshore crab varies greatly according to its locality, but it is most often a greenish-brown, sometimes with distinctive markings on the top of the shell or carapace. The crab approaching maturity adopts a much redder hue, so earning the nickname 'red belly'.

A short time before shedding takes place the new shell beneath has so cramped the crab's muscles that much of the power leaves its legs and claws. This is when the angler will find the vulnerable creature hiding under seaweed, around rock ledges, in soft sand and mud around rocks, harbour walls and breakwaters—anywhere which provides protection from strong tides and from natural enemies.

Artificial sanctuaries

Professional peeler crab gatherers often place broken roof tiles on the mud flats in estuaries or half bury tins in mud or sand to provide artificial sanctuaries—and thus traps—for the crabs. Gathering becomes much easier as these shelters are laid in straight lines, so decreasing the amount of walking needed.

(Above) Cornwall's rocky coast is ideal for gathering crabs for bait. Bass, like crab, are found feeding close inshore here.
(Above, right) Crabs can be hooked in different ways, while the legs alone also attract fish to the hook.
(Right) Small crabs can be bound to hooks by the use of the elasticated thread.

Of course, not every crab gathered in this way will be at the peeler stage. The only way to tell if it is suitable for bait is to carefully remove the end joint from a leg and see whether the segment has not been removed at all because the new skin is completely formed. If this is the case, the crab can go into the gatherer's bucket. It pays to collect more than will be needed for a day's fishing for they will be at different stages of moult and some can be kept for use when ready.

Having returned home, the angler should examine the bait carefully, selecting for use first those whose carapace has started to crack from the underside of the shell or those with a shell which has started to lift. The rest should be placed in a bucket of wet seaweed—bladderwrack is best—and kept in a cool place. These crabs will live up to two

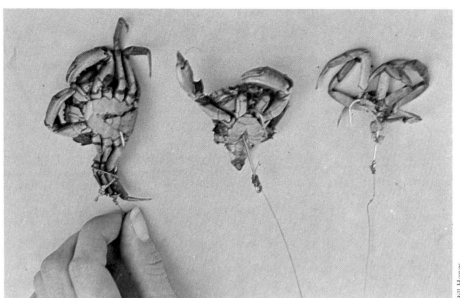

Bill Howes

Ken Whitehead

Many anglers hold that the peeler crab is the supreme sea fishing bait, while others criticise it because of the preparation needed. With care, however, several fine pieces of bait can be obtained from one crab. First remove the eight legs and two claws from the body and then, using the thumbnail, remove the carapace. With the aid of the thumbnail, or a knife, remove as much of the shell from the underside as possible.

Small baits

The crab can be used whole, depending on the size but, more often, the body is cut crossways in two or quartered to provide four small baits. Anglers often discard the legs and claws but these, hooked in a bunch like worms, can prove a deadly bait. By carefully removing the four segments one at a time from the legs with a gentle twist and a pull they can be peeled off. The claws can be dealt with in the same way.

When starting a day's fishing it is advisable to leave the peeler crabs in a bucket of sea water for a while as this makes them softer and easier to peel. Beachcasting crab puts considerable strain on this soft bait and so the whole body or segments should be tied to the hook with elastic thread or wool.

weeks, continuing the shedding process, but at a much slower rate than in their natural state. It is advisable to inspect them daily, removing any dead and renewing the weed after about a week.

A deadly bait

Peeler crabs are highly attractive to all sea fish but are especially deadly with bass and cod. Inshore boat fishing and beachcasting will both produce good results with this irresistible bait. The cod is greedy and is relatively easy to hook, but the bass will often suck the bait from the hook and so demands the angler's full attention.

Shellfish

In the sea, molluscs are a very important link in the food chain. Most important to the angler for bait are mussels, cockles, limpets, winkles and whelks. Many fish—the plaice is a typical example—will feed almost exclusively on baby molluscs, preferring 'seed' cockles and mussels. It is not surprising, then, that many species of shellfish have been used by the sea angler for many years.

Mussel as bait

The mussel, which is a bivalve, or two-shelled creature, has been a very popular bait for years, particularly on the East Coast. It is very easy to gather but it does require some preparation as it is virtually impossible to bait with the seed mussel upon which the fish are feeding.

There are about eight species of saltwater mussels found round the British coasts, but the horse mussel is the one generally used as bait by anglers. The young mussel begins life as part of the plankton before settling on the seabed and securing itself to rocks, stones, pier piles and similar spots with a series of very strong threads named the byssus. These threads, often called the 'beard', hold the mussel firmly to its rocky anchoring point even in the strongest gales. Mussels are sometimes found in great clusters and it is possible to gather a bucketful in minutes. It pays to be a little selective, picking out those with clean shells and leaving the barnacle-encrusted specimens, which are not usually as plump and juicy as the younger ones. The easiest way to remove the animal from the shell is to immerse in boiling water, which forces open the shell. The flesh is then removed by scooping out with a knife. Salt may be sprinkled on the bait to toughen the flesh and so make it stay on the hook. For beach fishing, a good method is to put three or four of the prepared mussels in a very fine-

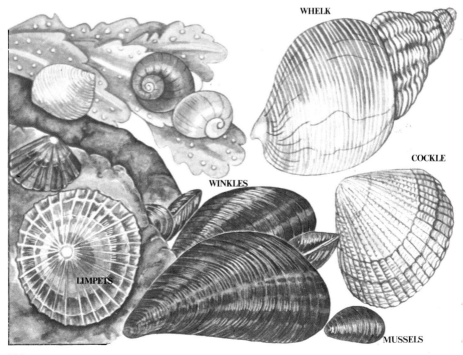

WHELK

COCKLE

WINKLES

LIMPETS

MUSSELS

1 *Limpets must be prised away from their bases by the use of a knife.*
2 *Single mussels are not big enough as bait, but a bunch makes an attractive offering.*
3 *By turning rocks over which are covered at high tide one can usually find a plentiful supply of hookbait from the animals which live there.*
4 *The whelk has a massive shell which has to be cracked open before the creature can be used as a hookbait. Once on the hook, however, its muscular foot holds it securely to provide an excellent bait.*
(Left) Most shellfish make good baits and the sea angler should be prepared to experiment with them.

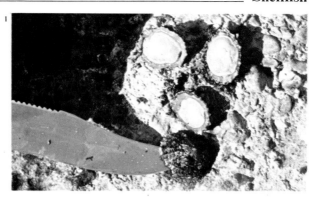

Ken Whitehead

mesh hair-net, which is attached to the hook and enables the bait to be cast a greater distance without flying off. Used this way, the mussel can be a deadly bait for cod.

Cockles as bait

Cockles are another variety of bivalve which will take many different species of sea fish. They are used extensively in Scotland, particularly on the Clyde. Cockles may take longer to gather as they have to be raked out of the sand in their preferred habitat of sheltered bays without strong tides or heavy surf. This bait requires no preparation other than the opening of the shell and the removal of its contents. Rather than cracking them open with a heavy blunt instrument, which will damage the animal inside, it is better to take a cockle in each hand, and where the

shells are hinged, lock one into the other and give a sharp twist. This breaks the hinge on the weaker of the two and allows the creature inside to be hooked out with the thumbnail. It is not a very large bait singly, but half a dozen or so on one hook make a very respectable offering.

The limpet is another mollusc, cone-shaped and dark brown in colour, which the angler can gather himself. They can be detached by prising them off with a knife or similar implement. The animal is then exposed and removed from the shell with the thumbnail, to reveal orange disc-shaped flesh and a blackish patch. Used singly on a small hook it is a good bait for flatfish, particularly dabs, while several on a large hook will attract most other species.

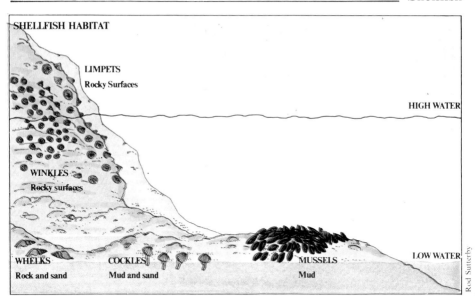

SHELLFISH HABITAT

LIMPETS
Rocky Surfaces

HIGH WATER

WINKLES
Rocky surfaces

WHELKS   COCKLES   MUSSELS   LOW WATER

Rock and sand   Mud and sand   Mud

Rod Sutterby

(Above) There is an abundance of marine life to be found where the shore is rocky, leaving small pools as the tide recedes. All shellfish here can be used as bait.

(Left) Barnacles and limpets carpet these rocks. When the tide comes in and covers them the limpets roam over the rocks seeking food. The mussels do not move, but their shells open and food particles are filtered from the gills to the mouth.

Unfortunately, its soft texture means that it cannot withstand forceful casting and is likely to be mutilated very rapidly by any crabs in the vicinity.

Where the winkle is found

The winkle, a member of the snail family, is among the smallest of the univalve molluscs. It can be found on most coastlines below the high-water mark and prefers a rocky bottom with good weed covering. The shell is smooth and ranges in colour from brown to black. The winkle is not widely used as a bait but fish are caught on it.

The main problem is that of removing the fish from the shell. If boiled first, this is done with a pin, but with a live winkle it is necessary to crack the shell with a hammer or any other blunt tool. As they are small,

several winkles are needed to make an adequate bait, but their toughness means that they remain on the hook for a long time and are not thrown off on the first cast.

The common whelk is much larger than the winkle and its flesh is greyish green. Large specimens can reach over 3in in length. They are to be found on seabeds of mainly stone and gravel and near the low-water mark at spring tide, but in considerably fewer numbers than the winkle. Professional fishermen take large quantities in baited pots from the deeper water and will usually sell a few to the angler. Again, the only successful method of removing the flesh while alive is to crack the shell, but one whelk makes a large bait, thus saving work and time in bait collecting.

Whelks are not really sought after as a bait by anglers, although commercial fishermen bait their longlines with them very effectively. Their success, however, can probably be attributed to the fact that a longline is left for several hours undisturbed and that the whelk is so tough that it will remain on the hook until eaten by a fish. For the rod and line angler it is best as a bait for cod and pouting as these two species are not particularly fussy.

Pirks and jigs

(Above) Pirks attract fish by the movement of their appendages as the lure is worked through the water.
(Right) A home-made 'baby octopus' cut from flexible plastic, with the head cleverly constructed from a drilled, painted, bullet.

In recent years pirking or jigging for free swimming fish such as pollack, coalfish and cod, has gained ground with deepwater boat anglers, and the method is now in wide use. It entails fishing with a weighted lure, invariably fitted with a treble hook. Pirks take many forms and range from lead-filled pipes, already chromed or painted in a variety of colours, to old plated car door handles or to sophisticated stainless steel and chrome-finished models from Scandinavia. Home-made pirks are cheap to produce, but the professional type can cost up to £5.

Jigs

Jigs are generally smaller lures, often with coloured feathers set in a metal head rather than the all-metal body of a pirk. They are

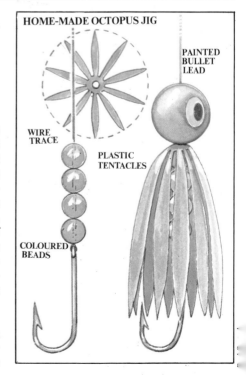

HOME-MADE OCTOPUS JIG

PAINTED BULLET LEAD

WIRE TRACE

PLASTIC TENTACLES

COLOURED BEADS

used in a similar way to pirks and range from 4oz to 26oz, the weight varying with the depth of water and the strength of tide. In general terms, few of less than 12oz are used in more than 20 fathoms of water.

Pirk fishing with heavy lures in the deeps requires a great deal of physical effort, which few anglers can keep up for more than half an hour. It is only with daily exercise that one builds the arms and shoulders to cope with the strain. Skippers who habitually fish wrecks in the Western Channel have the necessary physique and can keep a 26oz pirk going for hours on end, catching on average a hefty fish with every other drop. Tackle for this very specialized and rugged aspect of sea angling is a stout 7ft fast-taper hollow-glass rod, with plenty of power in the butt section. Matched with a top quality high-geared multiplier of at least 6/0, filled with 50-80lb b.s. monofilament line, such a rod will suit all occasions. Braided line is never used in this style of fishing because it creates too great a drag in tidal flowing water.

(Below) Pirks can weigh as much as 26oz, so fishing with them can be exhausting. But for wreck fishing, the fluttering, flashing pirk will attract big pollack in numbers. Sea anglers should always carry a selection, kept brightly polished.

When out with charter parties, most skippers stand high on the craft's bows, well out of the anglers' way, and hurl the heavy lure as far as possible, allowing it to flutter unchecked to the bottom. When this is done over a wreck which holds a big fish population, the pirk is often grabbed on its way down while still high above the wreckage. If not, it should be retrieved from the bottom ultra-fast, until contact is made.

Spring tides help cover ground

For really good fishing the boat must drift and cover as much ground as possible. West Country charter skippers, who have brought pirking to a fine art, enjoy the greatest success during big spring tides, when the flow of water carries their craft along at a speed in excess of four knots.

Pollack and coalfish are fast-moving predators, much attracted to what appears to be a tasty meal swimming for its life. Both species invariably take the lure with a sideways slash and the treble hook usually embeds itself on the outside of the fish's jaw. Quite a few become foul-hooked in the head area, in front of the dorsal fin.

Although small pollack in the 4-6lb class go for pirks, it is more often specimen size fish up to the record size of 25lb that are caught. A few years ago the author hooked a monster of 23lb 4oz on a large Intrepid

Mike Millman

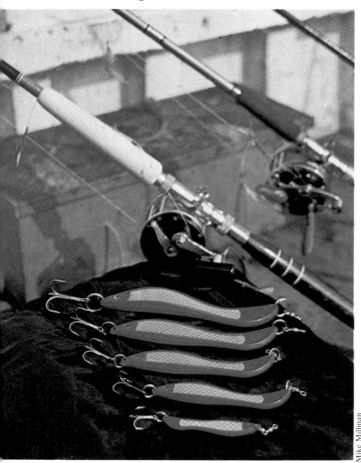

(Left) The Intrepid range of Flectolite 'Jiggas', blood-red deep-water pirks, from 1½oz to 16oz.
(Above) Home-made pirks. A yellow lead model and a tube filled with lead, both pirks drilled for split-rings and trebles.
(Right) Mike Millman with an excellent 20lb pollack taken on the lure seen protruding from the mouth of the fish.

Mike Millman

Flectolite pirk, at a depth of 42 fathoms. At that time it ranked as the fifth biggest pollack taken on rod and line, although coming from such deep water it had no chance to show its true fighting ability. Even so, pumping it up was not without effort.

It must be remembered, from a purely sporting point of view, that deep water pirking has little to offer. Tackle must be on the heavy side if the lure is to be worked correctly—and most fish are hauled un-ceremoniously to the surface without having time to make any adjustment to the sudden change in pressure. Unfortunately, not every angler is concerned about the sporting aspect. Growing numbers only want to catch fish, and that is a sentiment fully supported by those angling skippers who keep the bulk of the catch and sell it.

Anglers fishing pirks from conventional positions in a boat adopt a quite different approach to the quick retrieve method of the boatman in the bow, and instead work the rod with a pumping action, as one would with feathers. While it is effective if not more than six anglers fish at a time from just one side of the boat as it moves across the wreck, this method does not match the fast-retrieve system.

Baited pirks

The effectiveness of large pirks can be increased by adding 1ft-long, coloured plastic streamers (which serve also to hide the hook) and of course natural baits. A

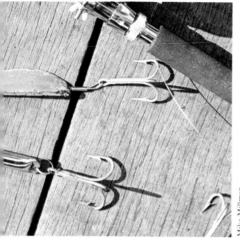

Mike Millman

Mike Millman

whole side of mackerel or cut squid does nicely. Both these baits are particularly good for ling, which hunt close to or on the bottom. Many outsize fish have been caught on baited pirks, including several weighing over 40lb from marks in western waters. Although one would not deliberately offer a baited pirk for conger, it is interesting to note that the former British record eel of 102lb 8oz, caught by Ron Thompson off Mevagissey, Cornwall, in 1974, was hooked by this method. Other conger weighing around 50lb have ended their days in the same way, in both deep and shallow water.

Pirking over reefs

Pirking over reefs and open ground, where the species are less numerous, is a different proposition. Here the drift fishing technique is even more vital to success. Cod are caught on pirks worked close to the bottom, particularly where the ground is mud or shale. In shallow water, pirking can be done from small boats or dinghies with much lighter tackle and baited lures of 4-6oz. The sporting element is high—cod hit lures hard and put up plenty of resistance by continually trying to bore down towards the bottom. Between 1970 and 1973 pirking for cod at the Ganntocks mark in Scotland produced dozens of specimen fish, some weighing over 45lb. Since then, the run of cod coming into the Clyde from the Atlantic

to spawn in January and February has shrunk noticeably. This is probably due to commercial trawling, which has been understandably heavy in the area. Despite this, good fishing is still to be had, with plenty of cod reaching double-figure weights.

The majestic halibut is in the true heavyweight class. The largest species of flatfish in the world, it frequents the Pentland Firth off the northern tip of Scotland and waters around Orkney and the Shetland Islands. Large shiny pirks of up to 3lb, fitted with tough, forged No 12/0 (and larger) treble hooks, connected to wire lines, have taken several monster fish.

Pirking for halibut

Drifting these large, purpose-made pirks close to the bottom in very deep water, where the tide is strong, is the most successful method for halibut. Landing a fish safely is another matter. Obviously, tackle in the 80lb class is needed before you stand any chance. But with a fish that can weigh 400lb, there is nothing unsporting about it.

Harbours and piers

Mike Millman

Fishing from jetties, harbour walls, piers and groynes into deep water has almost all the benefits of boat angling without that dreaded scourge of the angler afloat— seasickness!

Around Britain's varied coastline there are quite a number of seaward-projecting structures, providing an attractive habitat for a wide variety of sea species. Fish drawn to the security and food stocks of deepwater wrecks, rocks and reefs are also attracted to the underwater structures of piers, jetties, harbour walls and groynes, especially those in a good depth of water at all states of the tide. These provide abundant marine life in a natural state without suffering a drying-out process twice a day as the tide recedes.

Piers give moral support

Seaside piers have long been the favourite fishing stations for elderly, comfort-loving sea anglers, small boys and beginners who initially require the moral support and companionship of other fishermen as they make their first unsure casts.

One great advantage to young anglers fishing from above-water structures is that they can learn to operate their tackle by

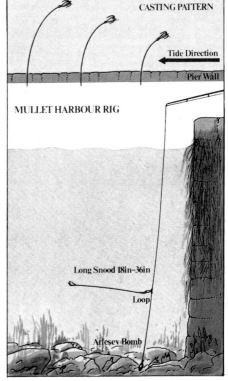

CASTING PATTERN

Tide Direction

Pier Wall

MULLET HARBOUR RIG

Long Snood 18in-36in

Loop

Arlesey Bomb

Rod Sutterby

(Left) Many tiny Cornish hamlets have harbours that are ideal for mullet and bass fishing. This is Charlestown, near the town of St Austell.
(Below) Harbour walls demand that anglers use casting patterns that respect all other anglers' fishing areas. Mullet fishing is best done by a long-snood rig.
(Right) For those anglers who suffer from sea-sickness, piers are the answer.
(Below right) With the paternoster, midwater and bottom species can be fished for using different hooks and baits such as lugworm and small dead sprats.

Bill Howes

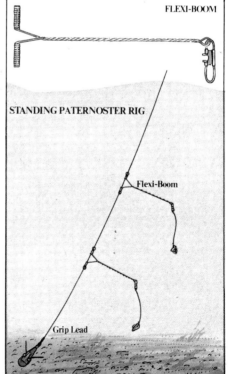

FLEXI-BOOM

STANDING PATERNOSTER RIG

Flexi-Boom

Grip Lead

Rod Sutterby

lowering it rather than casting. This eliminates 'crack-offs' and tangles when using multiplier reels.

The tackle should be powerful enough to cope with the conditions—such as the strength and height of the tide—as well as being strong enough to land the fish when caught. When float fishing for bass, for example, on the lower deck of a pier, it would be inadvisable to fish with 'open-water' tackle—a light spinning rod, a fixed-spool reel and 5 or 6lb line. The first good bass hooked would immediately dive for cover among the old barnacle-covered iron girders and smash such tackle. For such a snaggy angling situation, a stout beachcasting rod, a powerful multiplier or centrepin reel, and 15 to 20lb b.s. line is effective.

Where double figure cod weights are expected and a long haul-up has to be made, because the powerful rush of the tide makes dropnetting impractical, a stout pier rod about 9 or 10ft in length or a heavy duty beachcaster is needed, together with a powerful reel and strong line of 25 to 35lb b.s. Such tackle may appear to be on the

Harbours and piers

(Left) A number of fish species can be caught from piers and groynes. Bass, pollack and cod are taken in good numbers, but of them all, the mullet must be favourite. It is the speciality of the harbour angler, unknown by those who prefer the deep sea.

Mike Millman

(Right) One of the main problems about fishing from piers and groynes is that of getting large fish up from sea level. Your rod, reel and line will play the fish while it is in the water, but do not winch it up many feet to your level. Always have a drop-net ready for immediate use.

Bill Howes

pulley-hauling side, but it must always be remembered that with difficult shore fishing the strength of the tackle must be geared to overcome hazardous tackle handling, rather than just the fish itself.

Some seaward-projecting structures, however, present the gentlest of tides and sandy-bottomed fishing positions, necessitating the use of the very lightest of tackle—almost that used by the coarse fishing matchman. This is particularly true when fishing for harbour mullet which require a very subtle, silent coarse fishing approach.

A great deal of successful pier or harbour wall fishing can be done with the simplest of inexpensive tackle and a few fundamental terminal rigs. Provided the angler, who need not necessarily be highly skilled, studies the fishing conditions carefully, and presents the right bait when the fish are in a feeding mood (which could be at a certain state of the tide or during the hours of darkness—or both) good fishing can be had.

Long casting from piers is seldom necessary or absolutely vital to the making of good catches. Usually fish will be found

lurking in search of food around the underwater structure, right below the angler's fishing stance. A standard length 'pier rod', about 8–10ft long, will prove adequate when used in conjunction with a multiplier, a fixed-spool or a sea size centrepin reel. Short boat rods can also be used for pier and harbour wall fishing where the 'haul-up' is more or less perpendicular and there are no obstacles. If masses of rocks surround the fishing station and projections of various kinds present a definite hazard to the landing of a hooked fish, a longer rod will be of great assistance. This will enable the angler to steer his catch clear of the snags and haul it up, either directly with his tackle, or land it by means of a drop-net operated by one of his companions.

Match tackle with species

Line strength and hook sizes need to be matched to the size and species of fish expected. When the fishing ground is not 'tackle-hungry', for example, the pattern and weight of the lead used will be dictated by the strength of the tidal flow and the nature of the bottom which is being fished over. For general pier and harbour wall type fishing locations, where the usual catch may consist of the flatfish species—dabs, flounders and a possible plaice or two, small codling, whiting, wrasse, pollack, coalfish and the odd thornback ray and 'strap' conger eel—the main reel line could be fixed at a sensible 24lb b.s. and the rest of the terminal tackle scaled down in steps to minimize tackle losses. The reel line to lead link in such cases would consist of a length of 20lb b.s. and hook links or snoods of nylon 16lb b.s.

Paternosters are pier favourites

The favourite bottom fishing terminal rig for piers has always been the paternoster, where one or more wire booms are mounted above the lead. This method, if three booms are used with a hook dropper suspended from each one, gives the angler a chance to experiment with three different kinds of bait and the fish have a varied 'menu' to choose from. Hook sizes should always match the size of the bait being used so that it can be mounted correctly and neatly presented.

Vary baits and hook sizes

Where both large and small fish species are expected, the bait offerings and hook sizes can be varied so that a bottom-feeding flatfish can take a lugworm offering on a 1/0 hook and a double figure cod can engulf a small dead sprat mounted on a size 6/0 hook higher up the terminal trace.

Winter fishing from piers, harbour walls, groynes and jetties may necessitate the use of stout rods and strong line to combat rough weather as well as the energies of the fish. In the warmer spring, summer and autumn months, however, a great deal of fine sport can be had by employing light, fine tackle techniques.

Coarse fishing 'specimen hunting' gear is admirably suited to the pursuit of large bass, which in summertime, especially at night, forage around piers and harbour walls. Likewise, light float fishing tackle will account for the ultra-shy mullet, garfish and mackerel which sport around at dusk and after dark in the vicinity of groynes and jetties, especially if quantities of waste food,

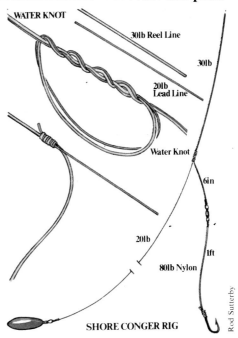

A shore fishing conger rig. The water knot is used to attach the 20lb b.s. leader to the 30lb reel line. A swivel leads to the 80lb hook trace.

vegetable matter or fish offal find their way into the water from fish quays or factories on the waterfront.

To avoid accidents and loss of life it is important that all shore anglers, particularly those fishing from angling stations above deep water, observe certain safety rules. Always observe strictly the rules of the pier or harbour wall so far as overhead casting, line strength and sinker weights are concerned. In rough weather, when waves are apt to break over the fishing station, leave the place well alone. On some piers, Tilley lamps and lanterns are banned because they constitute a navigational hazard when shone seawards.

Be careful when using a dropnet from piers or harbour walls with no guard rails and when climbing down perpendicular iron ladders or negotiating steep, weed-covered stone steps.

Harbours and estuaries

Fishing tackle, baits and methods used on exposed harbours and estuaries are similar to those used to cast from beaches and rocks on the open coast. With tide races and cross currents at their strongest at many harbour entrances, tackle must be even heavier than would normally be required for seafishing. Most harbours and estuaries, however, are quiet places where long distance casting and specialized tackle are unnecessary. For the beginner there are mackerel, garfish and flatfishes; for the more experienced angler the challenge of shy mullet and heavyweight conger eels.

Harbour fishing

To fish in harbours—or anywhere else for that matter—it is necessary to determine the fish's role in the environment. The next step is to use a suitable bait at the correct depth and location. It is pointless, for example, ledgering a strip of mackerel for mullet feeding on surface plankton. If mullet were taking pieces of bread from just below the surface you could assemble very light float tackle, bait with a flake of bread and cast near the feeding shoal. As mullet are shy it pays to cut line diameter to the safe minimum of about 4lb breaking strain; the rod and reel can be correspondingly light—a freshwater specimen rod and fixed-spool reel. The same tackle used with slightly stronger line would be suitable for the wrasse and pollack found closer to the seabed. Substituting worms and pieces of crab or fish for the bread should give excellent results.

Mackerel, garfish, bass and pollack are midwater predators that hunt their victims rather than waiting for them to drift past on the tide. They respond to bright, flashing movement and vibration which can be duplicated by a spinner of some kind. Artificial lure fishing is particularly good for these species when their activity cycles are at a peak; at dawn and dusk. Simple,

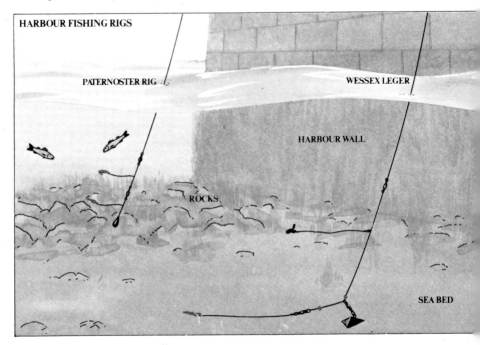

HARBOUR FISHING RIGS

PATERNOSTER RIG

WESSEX LEGER

HARBOUR WALL

ROCKS

SEA BED

lightweight tackle—freshwater tackle, for example—is perfectly adequate; even a simple handline may suffice. Successful lures range from spinners and spoons to feathers or even a strip of silver foil draped around a bare hook. The abundance of species that take either float-fished or spun baits probably explains why harbour and estuary fishing is so popular with holidaymakers and beginners. If a survey were taken, we would perhaps find that 90% of the seafish caught along the British coast are mackerel, small pollack and wrasse, bass and flatfish hooked from harbours during the holiday season.

Natural baits

Normal shorecasting tackle to throw the baits well out, so that they lie on the open ground, can be a helpful method. Worms, fish strips and sandeels attract rays, flatfishes, bass and even huge monkfish.

Fishing at night, when the fish are more active, is usually the best time when fishing off harbours. This is especially true when fishing for conger eels which hide during the day and are rarely tempted to feed. As soon as the sun goes down they creep out of the

Mike Millman

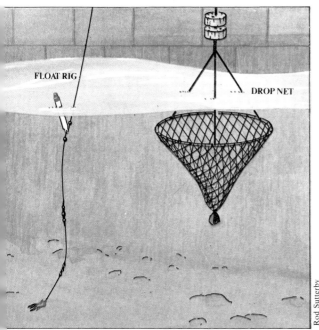

Rod Sutterby

(Above) The tiny harbour of Coverack, Cornwall. Many kinds of fish will come into this bay.
(Left) Many fish species, large and small, are attracted to the areas below harbour walls. In the summer, holidaymakers drop unwanted food down, fishermen throw small-dead fish and discarded bait into the sea. Offal may be thrown overboard from coastal vessels tied up. All this, plus the presence of natural food living on the weed and in crevices in the walls, encourages fish to stay. Drop-nets are used for hauling up large fish which may fall off the hook.

Harbours and estuaries

rock piles and weed beds and sport is brisk until dawn. Conger eel fishing is a rough, tough sport. Casting out a chunk of really fresh fish on strong tackle, wait for a bite, then be prepared to join in a tug-of-war—which the eel wins more often than not. But it is fun, offering chances to catch one of the biggest species the shorefisher encounters.

Estuary fishing

The species found in estuaries are usually the same as those in harbours and the angler may not be faced with long casting. There are, however, so many different types of estuary that it is impossible to generalize. The vast Essex Blackwater is little different from the open coast, having beaches, sandbanks and channels as well as creeks

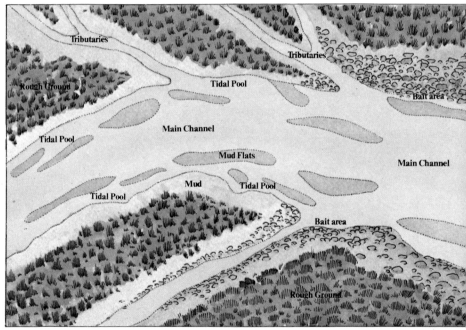

(Top photograph) Looking across the estuary of the Tweed from Berwick-upon-Tweed. On the far side lies Tweedmouth. It is a typical estuary, with prolific bait-gathering areas on acres of rich mudflats.

Estuaries are the homes of many species of fish. Bass, mullet, eels, gobies, garfish, flounder can all be fished for in the shallow, food-rich waters. Sea trout are found here on their way upstream to spawning grounds.

Off the main channel, mullet and trout, and eels too, will lie waiting for the tide to bring in food. The whole area is a natural food larder for all species and sea and land birds take full advantage of low water.

and mudflats. Some of the West Country estuaries, on the other hand, are no more than inlets used as harbours. As with successful fishing in harbours and from open shores, an understanding of natural history is important. If there are pilings, quays and backwaters, light tackle harbour techniques are best. Where there are sand spits and shingle beaches washed by surf, fish with standard casting tackle.

In estuary fishing the most significant factor which makes it different from other branches of seafishing is the fact that all estuaries are a confluence of fresh and saltwater. How they mix is crucial to the ecology of the area and therefore to the fishing. If vast amounts of freshwater pour into the estuary, as happens in a fast running spate river that tumbles from the mountains to the sea in a short course, seawater is swamped. The effect is to build up a saline gradient where the sea makes most headway in mid-channel but has little effect closer to the banks, where the water is brackish.

Some fish—flounders and mullet—are attracted to brackish water, but most of the truly marine species are repelled. To catch them you must fish from a boat in mid-estuary. Where saltwater dominates a sluggish freshwater flow and pushes it well inland, salinity is high even close to the banks and fishing is better for the truly marine species (cod, bass, plaice, whiting, conger eel) that require a high salt content.

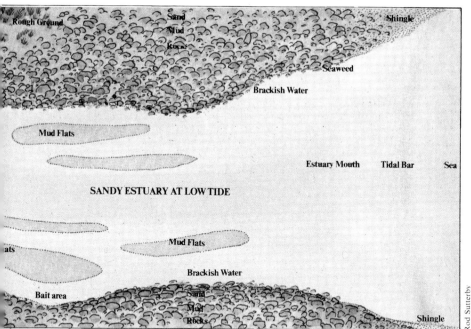

SANDY ESTUARY AT LOW TIDE

The main channel will hold the stronger bass, where they can feed on the lugworm and ragworm washed out of the mud and sandbanks by the force of the tide. Crabs, mussels, clams, cockles abound here.

As the estuary widens the water-flow slows and it is more shallow. Areas of weed hold small marine organisms such as shrimps and fish larvae. Still brackish, the water here has a greater salt content.

Many river mouths and estuaries often have tidal bars, where ridges of sand or shingle build into barriers that prevent the passage of craft. mackerel and garfish can be caught in this area.

115

Off-shore fishing

The off-shore fishing grounds round the British Isles have something for everyone. There are large skate, halibut, shark and conger, as well as cod, tope, ling, and a wide variety of lesser fish, all of which provide good sport on rod and line.

The secret of off-shore fishing is to know and understand the various species and their favourite habitats. For example, it will be a waste of time fishing over rocky pinnacles for tope. This small shark lives mainly by hunting flatfish and pouting, and usually confines its activities to flat, sandy or shingly ground. But pinnacle rocks are a good place to bottom-fish for conger, ling and cod. In mid-water around the pinnacles you will find the free-swimming fish such as pollack and coalfish.

Vital decision

Deciding where fish should be found is vital. Like people, fish will be found where the most food is available. Around wrecks or weed-covered reefs, for example, there will be a thriving population of small fish, crabs, prawns and immature lobsters. These creatures form the food of bigger fish, such as cod, ling and pollack.

All fish have good times and lean times. During the summer, shoals of mackerel and sand-eels provide a superabundance of food for larger species, and during the winter months, along the south and east coasts, huge shoals of sprat and immature herring drift inshore followed by packs of hungry cod, pollack and spurdog. This is good for the fish, but at times they can become so glutted with food that they completely ignore the bait, or are hauled sluggishly to the surface, their throats jammed with sand-eels or freshly taken sprats.

Seasons for sea fish

Anglers find that fish come and go through the seasons. In West Country and Scottish waters, huge influxes of coalfish and cod appear to mix with the ever-present pollack and ling. This leads to bumper catches. On the South and East Coasts, fish stocks have declined and anglers now rely on migratory species such as bream to provide good fishing. Off the Sussex coast, it is the April influx of good-sized black bream that everyone looks forward to, while a little later in the year, and farther along, off Hampshire and the Isle of Wight, anglers can find bass and tope, and perhaps even heavyweight cod during the winter. The same pattern applies right around the country with various species becoming predominant according to latitude.

Anglers seeking large fish—over 50lb —have more of a problem. There are fewer of them and as a rule their distribution is very localised. The conger is an exception, being widespread in southern waters. Halibut also grow to a large size, but fishing for them demands a trip to the Pentland Firth.

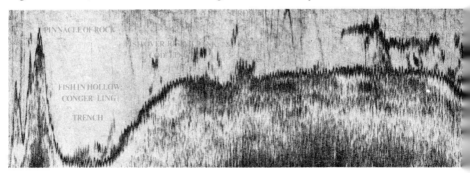

Bill Howes

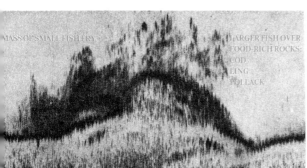

MASS OF SMALL FISH FRY

LARGER FISH OVER FOOD-RICH ROCKS:
COD
LING
POLLACK

(Above) This angler is holding his rod carefully away from the gaffing operation to avoid tangles. The monkfish is being properly gaffed in the jaws to prevent its edible parts from being damaged. A fish-box is handy to receive the fish.
(Left) Echo-sounders tell you where to fish.

117

As basic equipment, the off-shore angler will need a 6ft boat-rod. Longer rods are used, but as baited hook is dropped straight down over the side and there is virtually no casting to be done, length is not necessary to provide leverage for distance casting. Most boat anglers use the very effective multiplier reel which has a fast rate of line retrieve (useful when winding in from deep water), good braking, and a ratchet which enables the angler to prop his rod securely and adjust the brake to a correct tension so that a bite will be registered by the 'clack' of the ratchet. For off-shore fishing, line breaking strain (b.s.) should be about 20lb, although a stronger line should be used if you are fishing specifically for conger. In shallow water, when fishing for flatties, or out deeper for black bream, a lighter line will be adequate. But the 20lb b.s. line will stand a great deal of punishment if a sizeable conger is hooked.

One of the most effective terminal tackles is the running ledger, with the sliding boom holding a lead of sufficient weight to hold the bottom. This will depend on the strength of the tide. Leads come in all the standard shapes—grip, torpedo, bomb, Capta—and all do their job well when used at the right time and place. The running-ledger rig with boom, swivels, a two-yard leader and end

hook, will work well on practically all types of sea-bed, except rocks. Here some form of paternoster is necessary. With this rig, the angler will feel the weight hit bottom but know his hooks are placed above this. If care is taken to keep the sensitivity to a fine degree, with the lead keeping just in touch with the bottom, the hooks will not snag.

Try to keep your terminal rig as simple as possible. Apart from making the task of tackling-up quick and easy, it also helps to avoid a lot of wasted time when you have to unravel a tangle.

Tackling-up

Tackling-up is the first job, while the boat is heading out to the mark. First make sure that any items of gear not needed immediately—extra clothing in case of

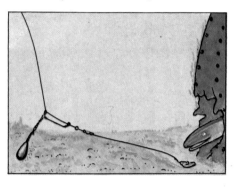

The off-shore seabed with its varied grounds and their fishing methods.

(Above) The ledgered bait will sit close enough to lure fish from the wreck.

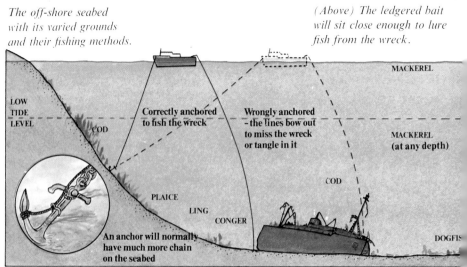

a squall, spare rods, food and drink—are all stowed away in the cabin, or somewhere out of sight. When fish are coming aboad there must be no unwanted gear to get in the way, especially if a conger is thrashing about in the boat.

Boat-owners do not look kindly on anglers using seat-boards or the gunnel for cutting up bait strips from mackerel or squid. Always use a baitboard and a sharp knife. Mackerel taken on feathers specifically for bait should be left in a bucket of sea-water or in a keepnet over the side in order to be kept fresh. This lively fish is by far the best bait for almost every type of sea fishing, and in the spring and summer a bout of feathering as soon as the boat is at anchor is advised. Sometimes a boat can halt on the

way out and be allowed to drift over a likely area for as long as it takes to get sufficient mackerel for the day's fishing. But don't assume that mackerel will always be around. So a standby bait—herring, squid, lugworm or ragworm - should be acquired before setting out. Most sea angling centres have tackle shops nearby which open early all through the week so that anglers can buy frozen baits and odd items of tackle.

Wait before dropping down

When the boat anchors, wait until the craft is steady before dropping down the lines. It may take a few minutes for the boat to sit right in the tide. Sometimes a small sail may have to be hoisted to hold the craft steady in the tide if the wind is coming from the side. The stern corners are the ideal places from

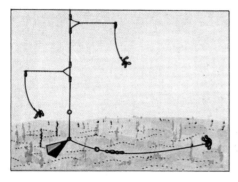

(Above) Paternoster tackle on the drift over sandbanks presents bait attractively.

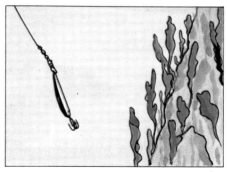

(Above) The pirk is a lure that works well while drifting over rocky pinnacles.

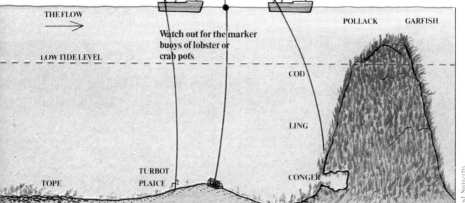

THE FLOW

LOW TIDE LEVEL

Watch out for the marker buoys of lobster or crab pots

POLLACK   GARFISH

COD

LING

TURBOT
PLAICE

TOPE

CONGER

Rod Sutterby

Off-shore fishing

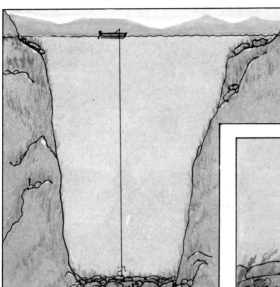

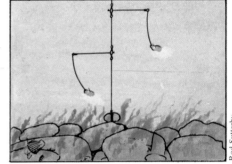

(Above, below) The many sea lochs of the Western Isles are usually so deep that fishing at anchor is impossible. Here, drifting is necessary, with paternoster tackle to avoid snagging bottom.

which to fish. From these places the lead can be of just enough weight to get the bait down, and then allowed to work out with the tide, but always being kept in contact with the seabed. The anglers behind them must have heavier weights to avoid tangling. The successful off-shore angler will adjust his tackle so that he is in constant touch with the bottom. He will not allow his lead to bounce up and down in the sand or mud because this will set up vibrations and echoes in the water that may well keep fish away. The ideal method is to be able to 'feel' the seabed all the time, and be able to differentiate between the small tugs and pulls of the tide and anchor-rope, and similar sensations from fish.

Don't snatch!

Different species of fish have different 'bites'. But as with other forms of fishing, it is not necessarily the biggest fish which give the strongest bites. Some large cod will give tentative pulls at first, but this fish has a very large mouth, so a hurried snatch by the angler may well pull the bait out of its mouth. Wait. Let the take develop, and strike when the cod has taken the bait, turned, and is swimming away. The hook will then be set properly and the fish can be played to the boat. Keep alert for bites at all times, but do not be misled by the very similar twitches which the tide can exert on the terminal rig. Experience will teach you the subtle differences.

Before setting out, whether in your own boat or not, be sure to have enough food and drink for the trip, a thick pullover and some weatherproof clothing. The day may be fine and the forecast good, but things can change rapidly in the long periods that sea anglers stay out—and especially if the fishing is good.

Remember not to anchor in a busy sea-lane; watch for the onset of a sea-mist; keep an eye on the sky. Squalls can blow up in minutes and the time taken to up-anchor may be just enough for real trouble to develop as the wind rises and turns a calm sea into a heaving and dangerous place for a small boat.

Be very careful to watch for the approach of bad weather. At sea, even close inshore, conditions can worsen very quickly. Do not hesitate to up-anchor and head back if this happens.

Seaway Code

Once you have fallen to the lure of sea fishing you may want to own a boat. But the sea does not allow many mistakes and before setting out in a boat of your own be careful to make sure you have a lifejacket. The *Seaway Code* is a useful little booklet giving helpful advice on safety for sea anglers, and can be obtained free from the Department of Trade, Room 306, Gaywood House, Great Peter Street, London SW1P 3LW.

Many fine pollack like this can be caught in the pinnacle-strewn waters off the rocky coast of Cornwall. A fish-box holds fresh mackerel caught for bait.

Len Cacutt

Wreck fishing

Wreck fishing is the most spectacular branch of sea angling and it provides anglers with the opportunity to consistently catch specimen fish. Reasonable catches are occasionally made from wrecks lying close to shore, but their accessibility can lead to overfishing and the numbers of fish living in them is drastically reduced. The best action is now found on sunken hulks lying more than 20 miles out, a distance which can only be reached in good weather conditions by skippers operating large, fully equipped, licensed charter-boats.

Some wrecks lying within ten miles of the shore are pin-pointed by using shore markers, but this is a chancy business. One skipper who made a success of this type of operation was Colin 'Fishy' Williams of Mevagissey, the 'man with the magic eyes', who had the incredible ability to anchor

(Left) Typical catch from a wreck mark.
(Below) The Decca Navigator and echo-sounder of a wreck charterboat.

right over hulks when the land was nothing but a mere haze.

The alternative is an electronic Decca Navigator, which receives a continuous stream of signals from shore stations. These are displayed as numbers on green, red and purple dials, which give an accurate cross-bearing of the boat's position in relation to 'lanes' on a special Decca chart listing hundreds of wrecks plotted by hydrographic surveys. Each hulk has a set of coordinates and when these are known it is possible to position the boat right over it.

Secret wreck marks

All charter skippers keep a record of the numbers and jealously guard them. Every year new wrecks are discovered by accident and as each is likely to be sheltering hundreds of fish, it is understandable that skippers prefer to keep such information to themselves. Some skippers go to great lengths to preserve the secrets of such a mark, only visiting the place when no other vessel is in sight. They then keep a vigilant

Mike Millman

(Left) 'Sunlit Waters', the well-known charter wreckboat at anchor in calm seas over one of the prolific Devon marks. (Below) Shark rods and reels must be carefully matched for strength, reliability and resilience against the huge strains put on them by hard-fighting conger and ling. The reels are 6/0 Penn and a 4/0 Tatler (bronzed).

Mike Millman

look-out during the time the boat is anchored over it, and should another charter boat be spotted they leave the area quickly.

Finding the wreck is one thing, anchoring accurately is something else. Many West Country skippers have brought this to a fine science and before letting the anchor go are able to take into account direction of tide, wind strength, and how the hulk is lying on the bottom.

Sometimes the anchor is dropped 600 yards uptide of the mark but, by the time the warp has taken up, the craft is close enough for baits to drop right back into the wreck where the fish are likely to congregate.

Dominant wreck species

While many different species are found on wrecks, the sport is dominated by conger, ling, pollack, coalfish and bream, all of which fall into three distinct categories. Conger and ling are taken on heavy-duty tackle and big baits ledgered on the bottom. The pollack and coalfish fall to medium-weight gear, artificial and natural baits, between the wreckage and the surface, although the bottom 10 fathoms is usually the productive zone. Black and red bream are caught by using more sensitive tackle or baits dropped right into the wreckage.

The techniques for catching each group will be discussed in turn.

Conger and ling reach enormous weights and over the past ten years records have gradually crept upwards. The record conger

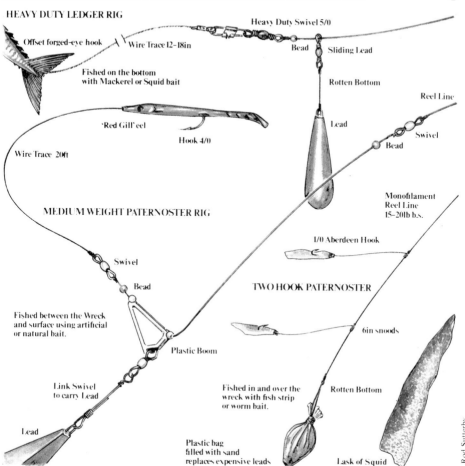

HEAVY DUTY LEDGER RIG

Offset forged-eye hook

Wire Trace 12-18in

Heavy Duty Swivel 5/0

Bead

Sliding Lead

Fished on the bottom
with Mackerel or Squid bait

Rotten Bottom

Reel Line

'Red Gill' eel

Lead

Swivel

Hook 4/0

Bead

Wire Trace 20ft

Monofilament
Reel Line
15-20lb b.s.

MEDIUM WEIGHT PATERNOSTER RIG

1/0 Aberdeen Hook

Swivel

Bead

TWO HOOK PATERNOSTER

6in snoods

Fished between the Wreck
and surface using artificial
or natural bait.

Plastic Boom

Link Swivel
to carry Lead

Fished in and over the
wreck with fish strip
or worm bait.

Rotten Bottom

Lead

Plastic bag
filled with sand
replaces expensive leads

Lask of Squid

Rod Sutterby

is now a giant 109lb 6oz, to the credit of Bristol angler Robin Potter, who was fishing 22 miles south of Plymouth. Britain's biggest rod-caught ling fell to Henry Solomons of Brixham, at a mark four miles south of Dodman Point, Cornwall, and weighed 57lb 2oz. Stout tackle must be used to deal with such fish successfully. The right combination for this heavyweight section of wrecking is a 50lb-test rod with a 6/0 multiplier and monofilament line. Braided lines are unsuitable for deep-water fishing as their drag demands the use of heavy leads.

There are many good British-made hollow-glass rods available, but when it comes to reels only the American Penn Senator and British Tatler models stand up

well to the terrific punishment wrecking imposes on fishing tackle.

Terminal tackle for these rough and tough fish is a ledger rig of good quality wire 12 to 18in long, ending in a 10/0 hook, preferably of the offset forged-eye type. A stout 5/0 swivel connects this to the reel line, and also stops the sliding lead from running down to the hook. It is good practice to use a rotten-bottom to hold the lead. This also obviates the need for a costly running boom.

Old or fresh bait?

Both conger and ling are catholic feeders, and will accept almost any fish bait, although the majority are caught on mackerel or squid. It is a half-truth that conger only take fresh baits, as many 50-pounders are taken

125

on mackerel three days old. But fresh bait increases one's chance of success.

The take from an outsize conger can be quite gentle in spite of its bulk and strength. It often mouths the bait for some time before actually taking it, and only experience will tell you when to strike. But never be in a hurry, for many conger hooked in the lips break free. When the rod tip tells you of the eel's presence the slack line should be wound in slowly until contact with the fish is made.

Get the conger into clear water

Once the hook has been struck home you must pump the conger into clear water above the wreckage. At this point, never give line, so the risk of being broken up must be taken. Later, line can be given under pressure through the slipping clutch. Conger weighing more than 50lb make continuous power-dives in an attempt to regain the wreck, while fish to 80lb have been known to dive back from the surface through 40 fathoms, despite a tight clutch and thumbs on the spool.

Ideally, conger should be brought to the

gaff in an exhausted condition. Failure to observe this important rule puts the catch at risk, and can be very dangerous for the chap wielding the gaff.

Ling feed quite differently and wolf big baits without any regard to caution. As soon as a bite is felt, the hook can be driven home, and the fish dragged away from the bottom. Fish weighing 30lb and more give a good account of themselves, but providing the hook has a firm hold, the issue should never be in doubt. After a few wreck trips the difference between conger and ling bites can be easily detected.

Wrecking for pollack and coalfish is tremendous fun. Both species are grand fighters and the line-stripping plunge of even a 15lb pollack is one of the most thrilling experiences in sea fishing. During the summer, most are caught on medium-weight tackle from anchored boats. The usual rig is a single 4/0 hook to a 20ft trace, worked from an 8in wire boom, or the recently introduced plastic variety. The boom effec-

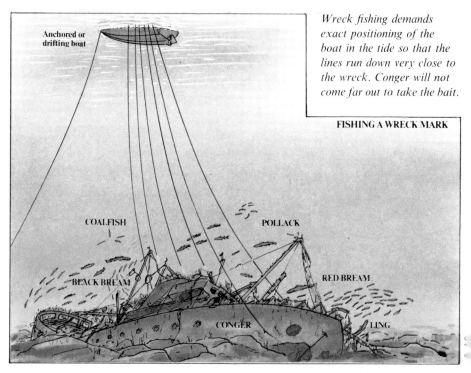

Wreck fishing demands exact positioning of the boat in the tide so that the lines run down very close to the wreck. Conger will not come far out to take the bait.

FISHING A WRECK MARK

Anchored or drifting boat

COALFISH

POLLACK

BLACK BREAM

RED BREAM

CONGER

LING

tively keeps the trace from tangling with the reel line during its long journey to the bottom. It is then steadily retrieved until the bait or artificial eel is taken. At this point the fish will make its characteristic plunge, and line must be given or a break is a certainty.

The coalfish is a better fighter because it is less affected by changes in water pressure. On the average it will make at least half a dozen tremendous runs before reaching the surface, and the fight is never won until the fish is safely in a net. Pollack, on the other hand, are much affected by the 'bends' and when pumped up too quickly arrive lifeless at the surface.

Mike Millman

(Above) A stomach pad is essential for helping the angler to fight strong plunges of big ling and conger hooked on wreck marks. The pad provides a pivot for the rod and takes much of the severe strain put on the angler's back and arms.

(Left) The rising streaks above the trace of this deep-water wreck show that there is a massive build-up of fish hovering above it.

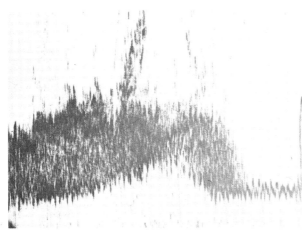

Mike Millman

Between November and March, females are heavy with roe, and so many fish congregate on deep-water wrecks that echo-sounders and fish-finders (sophisticated enough to normally pick out a single specimen) record what appears to be a solid mass. Most of the winter wreck fishing is done on the drift, after dan-buoys have been dropped to accurately mark the wreck's position in relation to the tidal run.

Spring tide = frenzied feeding

For several reasons, the best catches are made during spring tide periods, when the fast run of water stirs the fish into frenzied feeding activity. In this mood they strike fiercely at natural baits and various kinds of lures without hesitation. Big tides also ensure fast drifts across the wreckage, which makes it possible to get in as many as 30 productive drifts during a single tide.

Drift fishing is most successful when not more than six anglers work at a time. A charter-boat moves sideways down the length or across the hulk, and the lines stream out naturally from one side only. Working from the wrong side, the lines go under the keel. Apart from the obvious danger of cutting off, it is extremely difficult to have direct contact, and bring up the fish. Lines also tangle with those streaming away correctly, and much valuable fishing time is lost. It is a fact that too many leads plummeting down at the same time frighten fish, and the catch is often smaller when a 10-

strong wreck party are active all at once.

Most winter fishing is done with heavy-weight nylon paternosters rigged with artificial eels on short snoods. For a two-hook rig the nylon must not be less than 60lb b.s., and if three artificials are being used, which is typical rod-and-line 'commercial' practice, the strength is stepped up to 80lb. Even this can be snapped like cotton as two fish tend to run in opposite directions after taking the lures simultaneously.

Crude but effective

While the method of fishing is perhaps a trifle crude, it takes considerable skill to get the best out of it. The lures, weighted with at least a pound of lead, are allowed to plummet at high speed to the bottom. Quite often they are grabbed by fish swimming as much as 8 fathoms above the wreckage. When this happens, the multiplier is thrown into gear, and the full weight of possibly three specimen-sized fish comes on to the rod. The sudden, violent jerk is usually

enough to drive the hooks home, but it is as well to strike a few times yourself to make absolutely sure. At this stage, the slipping clutch is set to give line under pressure as the fish will immediately plunge downwards.

Successful winter wrecking on the drift depends greatly on the skill of the skipper. He must set each drift up to take advantage of the wreck's position and know exactly where the high parts are. As he watches the sounder, a constant stream of instructions is shouted back from the wheel-house, and the anglers must be ready to respond instantly to such orders as 'Up 50ft!' or 'O.K. We're over, drop back 50!'

Failure to heed the warnings will almost certainly result in the loss of tackle worth some £3.00. Repeat that a few times during the day, and winter wrecking becomes a very expensive business. Large pirks, or jiggers as they are also termed, fitted with large forged-eye treble hooks are used effectively for wreck fishing throughout the year, but a

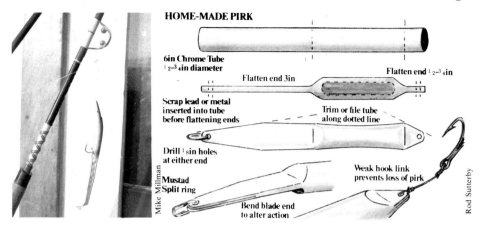

HOME-MADE PIRK

6in Chrome Tube ¹₂–³₄in diameter

Flatten end 3in

Flatten end ¹₂–³₄in

Scrap lead or metal inserted into tube before flattening ends

Trim or file tube along dotted line

Drill ¹₈in holes at either end

Mustad Split ring

Weak hook link prevents loss of pirk

Bend blade end to alter action

Mike Millman

Rod Sutterby

(Above) An artificial eel on a short snood for winter wreck fishing for pollack.
(Above right) Two rigs for wreck-fishing.
(Below left) The 'Conqueror' will become a great conger 'hotspot' for future anglers.

great deal of stamina is required to work a 26oz lure correctly for long periods. Charter-boat skippers, seldom short on physique, have developed this type of fishing to a fine art. Their method is to stand high on the bows, well out of the anglers' way, and cast the lure as far as possible, letting it run unchecked to the bottom. If it fails to attract a fish on its way down it is retrieved at an ultra-fast pace with a high-geared multiplier until it finds a taker. The largest pollack are taken on pirks, the author's best specimen weighing 23lb 12oz, which is not far short of the national record. Unfortunately such a fish hooked on a weighty pirk is quite incapable of achieving its fighting potential.

Tough on man and tackle

To cope with winter wreck fishing, tackle must be heavy, and it is customary for 50lb class hollow-glass rods and 6/0 to 9/0 multipliers to be used. Its tough on equipment, too, as many would-be record break-ers have found to their cost, when a rod has cracked under the strain, or a multiplier has jammed. Anglers also suffer: after the first dozen drifts and perhaps 20 big fish, stomach, arm and back muscles start pro-testing. More than a few men have been

exhausted to the point of giving up fishing, although down below fish were almost queueing up to get on a hook.

Normally, summer's black bream tend to stay around wrecks until well into December. The red bream record stands at an incredible 9lb 8oz, a fish hooked by Brian Reynolds of Plymouth, off the Dodman Point, Cornwall in 1974. By comparison the heaviest black bream is some way behind at 6lb 14oz, and was caught by John Garlick of Torquay in Lyme Bay off the Dorset coast, in September 1977. Both species are voracious feeders and many outsize fish have been hooked on large conger baits.

To get the best of bream fishing a most useful rig even for deep-water sport is a two-handed spinning rod matched with a light multiplier, for example the ABU 6000C or the slightly heavier Penn Long Beach 65, or Garcia Mitchell 624 models. End tackle can be a two-hook paternoster with 6in snoods made up from 15 to 20lb b.s. monofilament and 1/0 Aberdeen hooks.

For bait, squid is the best; it cuts well into thin strips and is very durable on the hook. Quite often several bream can be caught on the same bait, but as soon as the edges show signs of wear it should be changed. Other good baits for bream are mackerel strip and worms. All bites must be struck very quickly as sea bream have an uncanny knack of being able to strip hooks clean and can quickly eject those they consider suspicious.

129

Beachcasting

(Above) Herne Bay angler Ron Edwards in action in Ireland. (Below) Winter casting from a Penarth, South Wales, beach.

(Above) A left-handed beachcaster. (Right) Shore festival at Hythe, Kent. (Below) Start of a long-distance cast.

Really good beachcasters are disappointing to watch. The rod sweeps round in an effortless flick, seemingly without enough power to cast more than 80 yards. Yet this relaxed style will produce a cast of 150 yards.

Learning to cast is not easy, although there is no magic involved, no superhuman strength required and no demand for enormous talent. What you need is a basic understanding of the principles, well-matched tackle and sensible practice. Beachcasting 100 yards or more is demanding of time and effort, but anyone can reach this goal if he tries.

Casting is the transfer of power from the caster's body to the line and sinker. The rod merely acts as an intermediary to provide leverage. The sinker's momentum comes from its mass and speed, so for equivalent power a small sinker must fly much faster than a big one. As air resistance and other

drag factors increase with speed, it makes sense to use relatively heavy sinkers for long-range casting.

In good weather, 3-5oz sinkers give adequate carrying power but 6-8oz sinkers cut into gales better and tend not to tear soft baits from the hook. If weather conditions pose few problems it is best to use the sinker weight that suits the angler's physique. This must be found by trial and error by testing a range of weights between 4oz and 6oz in ½oz stages. Most people cast farthest with sinkers weighing between 4½oz and 5½oz. Regardless of the ideal sinker weight, as soon as the wind is in your face, change to a big, slow sinker to maintain range.

Sinker shape has little effect on distances—a chunk of scrap iron flies as far as a streamlined casting sinker. But the farther you cast, the greater the effect of tide pressure on the line. The sinker must anchor

130

Bill Howes

firmly in the seabed or the line sweeps ashore in a few seconds. In fierce currents grip-wired bombs are excellent, even at long range.

The trace is a source of drag and imbalance, both of which cut casting distance. Simple paternoster rigs are much better than running ledgers and just as effective for attracting fish. One hook is better than two or three, and all superfluous tackle such as swivels and booms can be dispensed with to save weight and cut down drag. Never tie the sinker directly to the line because the sand and shingle gradually weaken the knot so much that it will eventually snap in mid-cast. A split-ring makes an effective buffer and a very strong link. Wherever possible, present the most attractive baits, but if distance is the key to success, it is better to throw a second-rate bait the full distance than to offer a perfect bait 30 yards too short.

Line weight

The pressure of casting snaps ordinary reel lines and therefore a heavy shock leader is essential for beach work at more than 70 yards. Really powerful casters should use 35-45lb b.s. leaders for 3-5oz sinkers and 45-50lb b.s. leaders for the bigger weights. Ten yards of leader are sufficient for most casting and may be attached to the main line by a knot that will run through the rod rings with minimal friction. The main line can be much thinner than the leader because it does not suffer during the cast and undergoes very little strain in actual fishing. Nylon mono-filament of 15-20lb b.s. is ideal for all shorefishing except very light work and short-range, heavy ledgering for such tough species as conger eels.

Line length

As the amount of line affects reel size, it pays to use no more than the safe minimum. This is approximately 200-225 yards for routine ledgering, but fast-running tope need almost twice as much. The reel holding that much line is too big for really long casting but that seldom matters in tope fishing where fish are hooked at fairly short range.

For distance casting alone there is little to choose between multiplier and fixed-spool reels. The smaller reels of each kind are excellent for tournament casting to very great distances, but this is well in excess of anything possible from the beach. The multiplier is an all-round improvement on the fixed-spool, being better for retrieving, smoother, and more precise. Nevertheless, they are much more difficult to cast with, even if governed by casting brakes. Beginners are better off with a fixed-spool reel, because casting is enough of a headache without worrying about the reel as well.

THE SOUTH AFRICAN CAST

(Right) Leslie Moncrieff's original 'Layback' casting style used a stationary sinker and a very long rod handle. Now, tackle has shorter handles that allow greater power transfer. The stationary lead is given its swing (1, 2 and 3) and under the stress of the power stroke (4) the rod is thrust forward to position (5). So in both basic beachcasting styles the over-the-shoulder power stroke is all-important.

THE LAYBACK CAST

Apart from routine lubrication and cleansing, the only thing to remember about fixed-spools is maintenance of line level. Friction from the spool lip cuts casting range if the line level falls below $\frac{1}{8}$in from the lip when fully loaded. The importance of keeping the spool topped up cannot be overstressed. Correct loading of the reel will add up to 50 yards to a cast.

If sinker, trace, lines and reel are balanced, the design of the rod makes little difference to the newcomer to shorecasting. Use the shortest rod you find comfortable: 11ft for up to 5oz sinkers, a foot shorter for the bigger ones. Until casting range exceeds 150 yards with sinker alone, rod action is irrelevant provided that extremes are avoided. Ultra-fast tapers and reversed actions are too difficult to use when learning, and the beginner casts much better with a standard medium-fast rod. The rod's power is matched to the sinker weight and the caster's physique. The recommended weight range marked on the rod is a good guide but may underestimate the rod's potential.

Trial and error is the only way to evaluate rods. If you cast well and feel that the rod has just a hint of power in reserve, look no further. If it fails under pressure reject it, except for short-range fishing. Too much

(Left) In the South African cast the sinker lies behind the angler. *(1)* The shoulder swing begins at *(2)*, with the weight transferred to the left foot. Note that the sinker is still to the rear *(3)*. At *(4)* the power stroke begins, arms pushing and pulling, putting strong compression on the rod *(5)*. At *(6)* the line is released and the sinker can speed away, the angler aiming the rod-tip at the lead to keep friction to a minimum.

Rod Sutterby

power, which prevents the blank flexing fully, is disastrous because timing becomes far too critical for trouble-free casting. The most important specification is handle length. Unless the hands are about shoulder-width apart, full power is impossible and the casting action becomes stunted.

The best casts

The best casts for general beachcasting are the 'South African' and 'Layback' styles. Pendulum casts and all the tournament throws are too demanding for use on the open shore and impossible to use in the confines of surf and rock platforms. Simple casts are best, no matter how good the caster

might be. For beginners anything beyond these is a nightmare.

The South African cast, where the sinker is laid on the beach then swept over the shoulder with a twist of the shoulders and push-pull of the arms is an excellent teaching style and the foundation for all other casts, except the Norfolk methods. With properly matched tackle and sensible practice, the newcomer to shorefishing can learn to cast over 100 yards in less than three hours if he is instructed by a competent coach. Teaching oneself to cast takes longer, but a couple of weeks are enough to work out the details and to form the basis of a good style.

Sharking

Bill Howes

Most anglers assume that since sharks grow to a size much bigger than fish they normally catch their equipment must be scaled up and that it should be heavy and strong. Many anglers buy rods and reels with which they could fight and land fish many, many times greater than any that have been landed in this country. Many charter boat skippers also provide over-heavy tackle for those anglers without, who hire them for sharking.

Heavy tackle is not needed

Heavy boat rods, extremely large reels loaded with 130lb b.s. line are well beyond the requirements of any of our sharks since none make the fantastic 400-to-600-yard-runs of marlins and tuna for which such equipment was developed. Only very long runs require such heavy lines for the pressure of the water on the line during a long curving run (or its resistance as such a length is being moved through the water) would break a lighter line. Since the average angler can only produce a pull of 25lb with, say, a 7A, no angler would ever need a line much heavier than 30lb b.s. Moreover, the weight in water of any of our sharks cannot break the line, for the weight of the fish in water is only a fraction of its weight in air.

A fighting porbeagle comes to the gaff after being hooked from a shark-boat off the coast of North Cornwall.

Considering the fighting qualities of the various species liable to be taken, and the weight to which they go, the following types of tackle are recommended so that each would allow the fish to give the best sport:— blue shark—30lb-class tackle; porbeagle 50lb-class tackle; mako and thresher, as well as large porbeagle 80lb-class rod and reel. Each one of these tackle classes can be reduced to a lower one with increasing experience in catching shark. The terminal tackle, because of the size of baits used and the size of the mouth of sharks, should consist of large 6/0 to 10/0 good-quality hooks, attached to a biting length of 2 to 2.5mm diameter braided wire, because a shark's teeth are liable to cut through anything else.

The shark's abrasive skin

The biting length, 2 to 3ft long, should be attached to a further 10ft of slightly thinner, similar wire or long-liner's mono-filament nylon to withstand the abrasive action of shark skin.

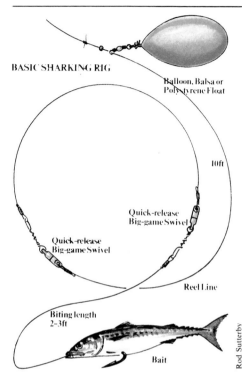

BASIC SHARKING RIG

Balloon, Balsa or Polystyrene Float

10ft

Quick-release Big-game Swivel

Quick-release Big-game Swivel

Reel Line

Biting length 2–3ft

Bait

Rod Sutterby

(Above) A standard shark-angling rig.
(Below) Shark tackle: Penn 6/0 reel, wire traces, big hooks and a float.

Bait in shark fishing consists of whole fish used either singly if the fish is large, or in number if they are small. The favourite bait is mackerel which as a shoal fish probably represents the commonest natural food of sharks. However, any other species may be used and many sharks have been taken on pouting or pollack. Various methods of mounting the bait are used with the head or tail pointing up the trace. Each method should ensure that the bait does not come off when first taken, for sharks rarely swallow the bait at once. Natural presentation is not essential, for the movement of the bait should give off the erratic vibrations of an injured or sick fish.

Bait—the off-the-bottom rule

Since sharks are usually mid-water or surface-fish, the bait should be fished off the bottom. This is achieved by attaching a float, either a balloon or square of polystyrene, to the line once the depth set for the bait has been reached. The float should always be as small as possible so as not to produce resistance once the bait is taken. This off-the-bottom rule on bait presentation is not absolute, for many sharks are taken with the bait on the bottom fished as a flowing trace.

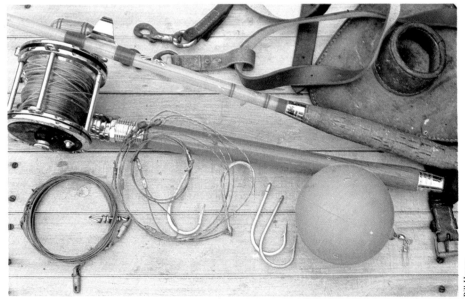

Bill Howes

TROLLING RIG

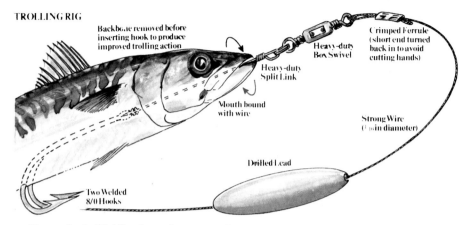

Backbone removed before inserting hook to produce improved trolling action

Crimped Ferrule (short end turned back in to avoid cutting hands)

Heavy-duty Box Swivel

Heavy-duty Split Link

Mouth bound with wire

Strong Wire (¹⁄₁₆ in diameter)

Drilled Lead

Two Welded 8/0 Hooks

The method of fishing depends very much on the area, the wind and tides, and both drifting and fishing at anchor are successful. In each case, the use of rubby-dubby is almost essential, especially if blue shark are sought. A good brew of rubby-dubby helps to bring the fish to the boat. Any shark swimming through its trail of fine particles will follow them to source and find the bait. The presence of the fine, oily particles of food prompts the shark into feeding.

Trolling for porbeagle

Recently, trolling a mounted whole fish bait for porbeagle has been successfully tried off Ireland. This is a standard method for mako in many parts of the world and would probably bring good results in British waters. But its one drawback is that only some four baits can be fished by this method. Its obvious advantage is that a much greater area can be covered. Line must be paid out as soon as the bait is taken so that the fish has a chance of swallowing the bait before the hook is set. No rules can be made about striking. While some sharks will take the bait with a rush, others will play with it before taking it properly, or perhaps leave it alone. In every case, should a strike be missed it is advisable to retrieve the bait slowly with frequent stops. This may induce the shark to have a second go, providing always that the hook is not bare.

Similarly no rules are possible about the

type of fight to be expected. In many cases it will not start until the fish has been brought to the side of the boat for the first time. After this anything may happen, long runs away and towards the boat, periods of inactivity or deep soundings. Two species, the mako and the thresher, will make long runs and will often clear the water completely in repeated, spectacular leaps. But the fish will tire slowly and come to the side of the boat. At this stage it may suddenly sound, or stop fighting altogether. On being brought to the surface such fish have often been found to be dead. Once a fish is really tired, then, and only then, should be the time to bring it inboard

(Above left) Before mounting on the double-hook, the fish's backbone should be removed. The bait will then have a good, realistic action while being trolled.
(Left) Beneath the burgee of the Shark Angling Club of Gt Britain, five small flags indicate the number of shark that had been caught in the day's outing.
(Right) Two gaffs are needed to lift this defeated porbeagle into the shark-boat.
(Below) Trolling for porbeagle, using a group of teasers—mackerel with their backbones removed. This method was first tried, with success, by Leslie Moncrieff and Mike Prichard.

Bill Howes

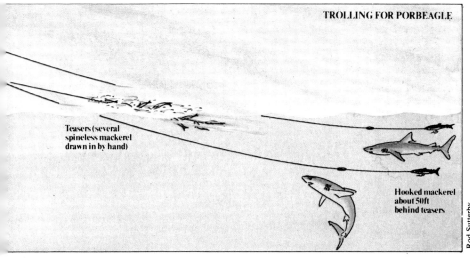

TROLLING FOR PORBEAGLE

Teasers (several spineless mackerel drawn in by hand)

Hooked mackerel about 50ft behind teasers

Rod Sutterby

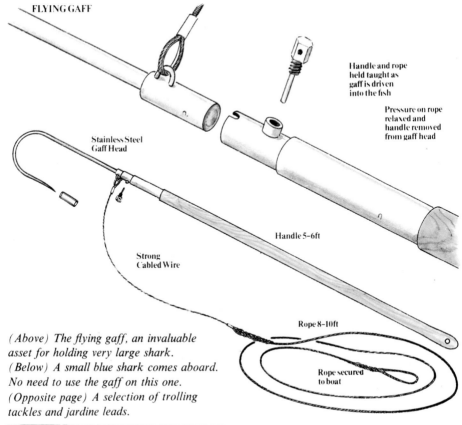

FLYING GAFF

Handle and rope held taught as gaff is driven into the fish

Pressure on rope relaxed and handle removed from gaff head

Stainless Steel Gaff Head

Strong Cabled Wire

Handle 5-6ft

Rope 8-10ft

Rope secured to boat

(Above) The flying gaff, an invaluable asset for holding very large shark.
(Below) A small blue shark comes aboard. No need to use the gaff on this one.
(Opposite page) A selection of trolling tackles and jardine leads.

Mike Millman

for a lively shark can do great damage to an angler or a boat. Always fight a shark in the water—not in the boat. Small sharks can easily be lifted into the boat by hand if the freeboard of the boat is not too high.

The flying gaff

The use of flying gaffs, those which have detachable handles where the head itself is attached to or carries a rope, is essential, since most gaffed shark thrash about wildly. They are then easier held at the end of a rope and there is less chance of injury from the handle which may break or be moved around erratically by the thrashing fish. A noose passed over the tail of the fish lying at the side of the boat can also be used to tether the fish. This is probably the best method as it always allows the fish to be returned to the water uninjured, necessary if anglers are to continue to enjoy their sport.

Sea trolling

Trolling or towing a bait, natural or artificial, behind a moving boat to catch fast-moving predatory fish, has been practised for centuries. There exist in museums in North America polished stone rigs used by Eskimos as long ago as the 15th century.

Up to the late 1950s trolling was one of the principal fishing methods used by sporting anglers in British waters. Then, when charter boats fitted with sophisticated electronic equipment came onto the scene, sea angling underwent massive changes. The opportunity to make large catches quite easily from an anchored boat on wreck marks proved too great an attraction for many anglers, and trolling, or whiffing as it is sometimes termed, was almost forgotten. To be fair to trolling, the method was only suitable for the angler with his own boat, or with access to a small craft, so perhaps it was

natural that the new sport of wreck fishing became so popular.

At present, however, there is a definite swing back to the use of small boats, for anglers tire of four-hour runs out to a mark and do not welcome the high cost of a day's fishing. Besides, certain species—bass, for example—could never be caught from a charter boat with ten anglers aboard, and so devotees have continued to fish as their forefathers did, although technical advances are making a great difference to the catches.

Varied baits

Baits for trolling are very varied. Small whole mackerel and sandeel are widely used, as are mackerel and squid strip. Marine worms are used to a lesser extent. Bright metal lures fitted with treble hooks are popular, but their effectiveness is largely restricted to shallow water fishing for

Mike Millman

(Right) Two very good trolling baits. The squid is mounted on a double hook, with strong threads providing struts to ensure that the wings adopt a natural attitude. The 'cocktail' rig consists of a red plastic squid and a dead herring mounted close behind it.

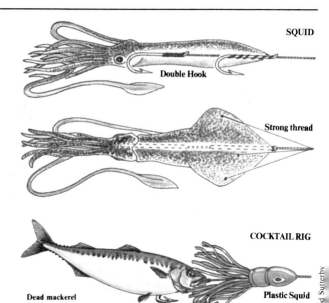

SQUID

Double Hook

Strong thread

COCKTAIL RIG

Dead mackerel

Plastic Squid

Rod Sutterby

mackerel, pollack and school bass. In deeper water the artificial eel is now generally used with great success. Lures of this type have come a long way since the introduction of the first models, which featured a plastic body and a tail made from the rubber ring of a jam jar. Thirty years of steady development have brought considerable manufacturing expertise, yet improvements continue to be made.

Red Gill

Red Gill, the brainchild of Alex Ingram of Mevagissey, is now a fourth generation lure. His latest innovation is a specially shaped hook, fitted to the large Thresher model, which prevents the body of the lure being detected and pushed up the line, when a fish strikes at it. Of the five models offered the 172mm size is by far the most successful.

In the last couples of years, however, the Eddystone Eel, produced by David Beer of Plymouth, has proved a serious rival. It has a much softer tail made from ultra-thin plastic, which gives a faster action, making it particularly suitable for trolling at slow speeds without losing its attractive motion. The Eddystone Eel is available in a number of sizes, but the medium model of 190mm gives the best results.

A new lure, the Eddystone Troller, which has an all-through action will possibly be the best yet. This lure was the result of an enormous amount of research, done with the cooperation of the expert bass anglers who fish Eddystone, Britain's top bass mark. The spectacular catches are made over the gullies close to the lighthouse itself, where giant bass, some weighing as much as 20lb, are common. But catching them has proved impossible so far.

Artificial eel

The best rod and line capture made on an artificial eel is the British record bass of 18lb 14½oz taken by Roy Slater in 1975. The biggest fish are extremely wily, and refuse to be tempted by anglers' lures, but hundreds of fish weighing between 7 and 14lb are taken each year. To contact them requires a thorough knowledge of the reef, for the only way they can be caught is by trolling the lure at least 100 yards behind the boat, taking it right through the jagged gullies. The rocks on either side rise to within a foot of the surface, and even a slight knock against the gneiss rock will hole the stoutest craft.

The bass anglers at the Eddystone, rightly known as the most dangerous reef in the

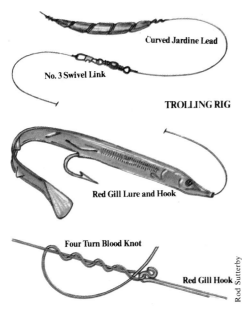

Curved Jardine Lead

No. 3 Swivel Link

TROLLING RIG

Red Gill Lure and Hook

Four Turn Blood Knot

Red Gill Hook

Rod Sutterby

(Left) Swivels are an essential part of trolling rigs. Without them lines will become hopelessly twisted.
(Overleaf) Trolling off the unmistakable Eddystone rocks.

average weight. The best patterns for trolling are those whose centre of gravity is below the level of the line, which prevents twisting or kinking. A curved jardine lead is mounted by running the line around a continuous groove and spiral wires at the ends of the lead. This kind can be changed without cutting the line and is very popular for that reason.

Trolling for pollack

Trolling for large pollack on offshore reef marks requires a similar approach. During the day, the fish swim near the bottom, so trolling is best at first light and in the late evening when they rise to within a few feet of the surface. As with the bass, it is vital to work the bait a long way behind the boat, where it is well out of the way of engine noise and propeller turbulence.

Working a lure for these 'race' pollack is an exciting sport, and records prove that trolling is one of the deadliest methods for making big catches. An indisputably classic haul was made many years ago, when Captain and Mrs H Millais trolled rubber eels 6ft below the surface at $3\frac{1}{2}$ knots, off Sennen Cove in the far west of Cornwall.

Their first session, in the early evening, produced 24 pollack and coalfish, weighing 269lb, which included a pollack of 21lb and a 20lb coalfish, at the time the biggest ever caught on rod and line. The following evening saw a repeat performance, when 34 fish totalling 416lb came to the net. The best specimen was a coalfish of 23lb 8oz, which was to hold the British record for a great many years. While these were exceptional catches, there are many instances of hundreds of pounds of fish being taken, at times in a matter of hours.

Shallow water

Fishing shallow water close to a rocky shoreline can be very rewarding, especially during the later months of the year, when

English Channel, fish alone, and this presents problems. To leave the tiller or wheel for just a moment in the turbulent waters when the boat is under way, even at three knots, is asking for trouble. To avoid it, rods up to 15ft long and fixed to special holders mounted in the stern are used. When a bass hits the lure, the length of the rod first cushions the powerful strike and then its spring back, combined with the boat's forward speed, drives the hook home. At this point the boat's engine is knocked out of gear, leaving the angler free to net the fish.

The experts have tended, in the past, to use lures of their own design, jealously guarding their secrets. Tempers have risen sharply when lines have crossed and one angler has wound in and seen the other's lure. Home-made varieties are now less common but a few anglers still modify commercial lures in various ways in the hope of gaining the edge over rivals.

Usually two rods are used at once, and these are matched with multiplier reels filled with 35lb b.s.monofilament line and 25ft traces of 25lb b.s. The size of lead depends on the strength of tide, speed of the boat, and depth the lure is to be fished, but 1lb is the

bass and pollack hunt inshore. The best places to search for them are in the tide rips off headlands. Fine examples that spring readily to mind lie close to Berry Head, in Devon, and Rame Head, Dodman Point, and the Lizard in Cornwall, at all of which big catches are regularly made.

It is best to troll in the early morning, and locals who specialize in this type of fishing are generally afloat by 6.30am and reckon to have half a dozen good bass in the bag by breakfast. The same trolling tactics are used for fishing close in, but it seems that natural baits, particularly sandeels, catch better in shallow water. Used in a live state, and trolled at very low speeds, success is assured.

Hooks
Eels should be mounted on long shanked fine wire hooks such as the Aberdeen, by passing the hook point through the fish's bottom lip and then nicking it into the soft skin on the underside just behind the head. Presented in this way on a long trace, the eel can swim naturally and will live for some time, thus avoiding the need to change the bait.

Although discussing trolling, it is worth mentioning that live sandeel mounted in the manner described, but offered on a split-shotted 20ft long drift line, as the boat moves along with the tidal run, is a superb method of attracting bass and pollack.

Lifelike movement
Returning to trolling with dead sandeel, it is essential for the eel to be very soft and flexible, so that its movement in the tide will be lifelike. This is best achieved by gently bending the fish backwards and forwards until the backbone is broken in a dozen places. Some anglers prefer to use a thin strip from the length of the sandeel, which is hooked through once at the thickest end of the piece. It is essential to cut the strip evenly, using a thin-bladed, razor-sharp knife. Any suggestion of a jagged edge will spoil the movement and this will be instantly spotted.

Sea birds are a good indication of fish feeding near the surface, constantly wheeling and diving over the water. Find them, and you stand a good chance of coming home with a fine catch.

Mike Shepley

143

Feathering

MACKEREL FEATHERS

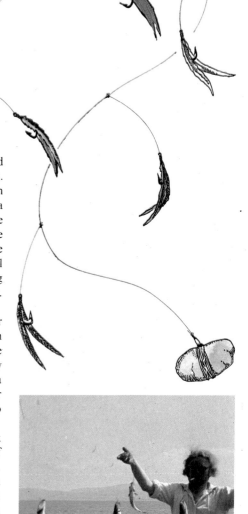

Hooks dressed with feathers are often used to catch mackerel, pollack, cod and whiting. Less commonly, bass and garfish are taken by 'feathering'. The tackle is set among a shoal and jerked up and down to simulate the erratic movement of small fish. The use of several feathered hooks helps create the impression of plentiful food. Once a shoal has been located a greedy mackerel, whiting or codling can often be taken on each hook.

Boat or pier

This technique has been employed for generations in Scottish and North Eastern coastal waters, but has now spread to the South. Feathering is most frequently practised from a boat, using either a rod or a handline, wherever shoaling occurs. Pier anglers, again using either tackle, can also take advantage of incoming shoals.

The rig for feathering consists of up to six feathered hooks on traces or 'snoods' of about 5in, which are attached to the reel line. A line of 15-20lb b.s. should be used, for with a fish on every hook it will have to take a considerable load when being reeled in to a boat or a pier. The snoods should also be strong enough to avoid losing any fish when hauling in the catch and should be set 9-10in apart so that they do not tangle. A fairly heavy lead should be used at the end of the reel line, for a smaller weight may take a long while to sink, by which time the shoal may have moved on, the feathers not having had a

Bill Howes

144

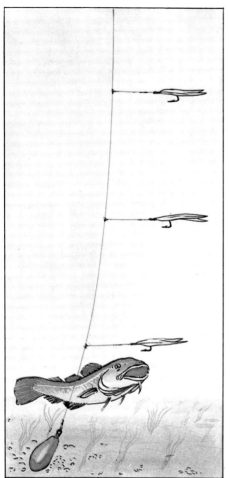

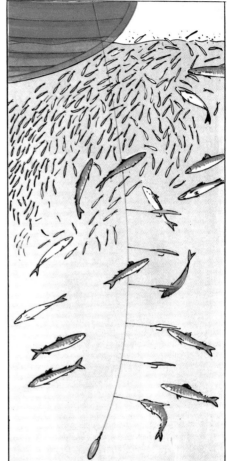

Rod Sutterby

(*Left and above*) *Mackerel can be taken in large numbers on six-hook feathered traces. The feathers, coloured, resemble small fish.*
(*Right and above*) *Cod feathers come from white chickens. While they can be 'worked' in the way mackerel feathers are pumped up and down, cod can be caught by allowing the feathers to stream out. Some commercial fishermen have feather winches.*

Bill Howes

Feathering

Bill Howes

(Left) When you find them, mackerel come inboard in large numbers. Those that are not needed for bait can be gutted and taken home. Do not, however, assume you will catch enough for the day's fishing, so take a standby bait along, such as frozen fish, squid or lugworm. (Right) Both mackerel and cod feathers can be bought quite reasonably from your local tackle shop. But feathered traces can be made simply. The whip-knot is an easy one to tie by following our numbers from 1 to 5. When the line is pulled through the last winding, make sure that all the turns are close and neat before pulling both ends tight and cutting off.

BAITED FEATHER RIG

Bead

Flexi-boom

Bead

A baited and feathered hook can attract fish. The gleam from mackerel skin, plus the waving feather, is a good fish attractor.

Spade whip

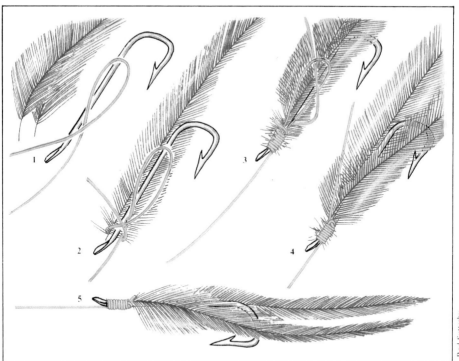

Rod Satterby

chance to attract them. For mackerel a size 1 or 1/0 hook is suitable; for cod a larger hook, a 3 for example, is recommended.

When fishing for mackerel as bait (which is hard to beat for its appeal to many species) a six-hook rig will provide a plentiful supply. A group of boat anglers must remember though to be careful when swinging these multi-hook rigs in board, especially in a wind, for painful accidents and lost fishing time can result from lack of forethought.

Three feathers only

The taking of large catches of mackerel in this way—and they are extremely easy to catch—is regarded by some as unsporting, and is very wasteful if, as is often the case, many fish are killed when not needed for bait or food. This is all the more serious when the mackerel, like other species, is being depleted too rapidly by the growth of commercial fishing.

In any case, when the acquisition of bait is not the objective, the sport achieved with a single feather, especially one made to one's own design, is much more enjoyable. Combine this rig with a lighter rod and line for best effect. Single feathers provide a good opportunity for experimentation and, with practice, for fishing selectively. Bass, for example, have been caught on a lure made from a salmon fly' to which two white feathers are added.

When fishing for larger species such as cod and pollack, it is impractical to use more than three hooks as the weight of these fish makes them considerably more difficult to boat than mackerel or whiting.

Traces of feathers can be bought ready-made from tackle dealers, but it is cheaper to make them yourself, using chicken feathers. These, taken from the neck, where the length and quality are best, are used in their natural white or can be dyed, usually in bright shades of blue, green, orange or red. They are whipped firmly onto sea hooks of a size appropriate to the fish sought, and are then ready to be attached to a snood made from the reel line.

Weather

Weather plays a vital role in every aspect of sea angling, and to treat it with less than total respect is asking for trouble. Most commercial fishermen, like men who work the land, can predict with uncanny accuracy what the weather pattern is likely to be half a day ahead, simply by looking at the sky. Unfortunately, it takes years of experience, and ordinary folk must rely on more down to earth methods of forecasting, and what is known as the Beaufort Scale or Wind Force.

This was devised in the early 19th century by Sir Francis Beaufort, a British naval officer and hydrographer, and classifies wind speeds ranging between Force 0—Calm, and Force 12—Hurricane. This is now the standard scale used in meteorology, and gives a good guide as to what conditions may be expected in the open sea. A knot is the measure of the speed of ships and is equal to one nautical mile, or 6,080ft, per hour.

It should be realized that the Beaufort wind scale chart can only be a guide as to what might be expected in the open sea. Should the direction of wind be against the run of tide, even a moderate Force 4 can put up a much fiercer sea locally. Facts such as this must always be taken into consideration

Weather condition	Wind speed	Wave height
Force 0 Calm. Sea like a mirror.	Less than 1 knot	
Force 1 Light air. Sea has a series of ripples.	1–3 knots	Not more than 3in.
Force 2 Light breeze. Small short waves appear. Crests have a glassy look and do not break. Usually good fishing weather.	4–6 knots	About 6in
Force 3 Gentle breeze. Large wavelets seen. Crests begin to break. Foam of glassy appearance with a few 'white horses'.	7–10 knots	About 2ft
Force 4 Moderate breeze. Small waves becoming longer. 'White horses' constant.	11–16 knots	3½ft
Force 5 Fresh breeze. Moderate waves very much longer in form. 'White horses' everywhere. Spray starting.	17–21 knots	6ft
Force 6 Strong breeze. Large waves with extensive white crests form. Abundant spray.	22–27 knots	9½ft
Force 7 Near gale. Sea heaps up and white foam from breaking waves blown in streaks along the direction of the wind.	28–33 knots	13½ft

Force 0: A flat-calm Skye seascape, but sadly rare in those rugged waters.

Force 1: Gentle ripples, light air—but note the Warm Front cloud pattern.

Force 8 Gale. High waves of greater length. Edges of crests begin to break in spindrifts. Foam blown in well-marked streaks along direction of the wind.	34–40 knots	18ft
Force 9 Strong gale. High waves, dense streaks of foam blown along. Crests of waves begin to topple, tumble, roll over. Heavy spume affects visibility.	41–47 knots	23ft
Force 10 Storm. Very high waves with overhanging crests. Resulting foam, forming great patches, blown into dense white streaks. Surface takes on a white appearance. Violence of the sea becomes heavy and shocklike. Visibility much affected.	48–55 knots	29ft
Force 11 Violent storm. Exceptionally high waves. Small and medium sized vessels might be lost for a time behind the troughs. Sea completely covered with white foam. Everywhere the edges of the wave crests are blown into froth. Visibility badly affected.	56–63 knots	37ft
Force 12 Hurricane. Sea a maelstrom of spray and foam. Becomes completely white, affecting visibility very badly.	64 knots or more	In excess of 37ft

Weather

Bill Howes

Richard Jemmett

Force 2: A pleasant breeze on a hot summer's day. No weather trouble.

Force 4: White horses everywhere here, looking out from Weymouth Harbour.

when embarking on a deep water outing, or indeed on any kind of boat fishing trip.

Influence of the land

The contour of the land can also have a big bearing on the condition of the sea, even miles offshore. For example, a near westerly gale in the western English Channel will keep water angling boats operating out of Fowey, Looe, Plymouth, Brixham and Torquay tied up to the quay, but their counterparts at Falmouth and Mevagissey will be afloat over wreck marks lying in the vast area of Falmouth Bay. The reason is the influence of the Lizard Peninsula, which stretches out for miles, almost due south, from the Cornish coast. This gives so much shelter that it is possible to fish in comparative comfort 10 miles off the land, while just a mile to the east the sea will be a maelstrom of white water.

Estimating wind force

In estimating wind force from the appearance of the sea, factors such as depth of water, swell and the effect of heavy rain, which tends to flatten the sea, must be noted. The latter can easily give a false impression of the sea's true state. It is also impossible to estimate the wind at night by sea criteria. Near land or in enclosed waters with an offshore wind blowing, wave height will be much smaller and the waves steeper.

If you make a booking for a deep water trip on a licensed craft operated by a professional skipper, the worry of whether conditions are suitable for fishing can be left

to him. Above all, do not question his decision to cancel the trip you have been looking forward to for months. He will have done so with great reluctance after taking detailed advice from the local meteorological office. Remember that he makes a living by going to sea and that staying tied up to the wharf unnecessarily will not pay the rent and keep an expensive boat with hired electronics in operation.

Through thousands of deep water angling trips in the past decade the sport has retained a 100 per cent safety record—professional skippers want to keep it that way.

Don't chance it—stay at home!

Unfortunately, the same cannot be said for privately owned craft. Every year anglers lose their lives in boating accidents, simply because they did not have the common sense to stay ashore when bad weather was forecast. Indeed, many are stupid enough to set out in conditions that are already dangerous—an act which all too often puts at risk the lives of those engaged in subsequent rescue operations.

Small, open boats are unsafe in winds of Force 3 and upwards, and under these conditions should never be taken outside sheltered water.

Most local authorities and harbour masters post detailed local weather forecasts outside their offices. A forecast can also be obtained from the nearest meteorological office or by dialling the GPO Telephone

Force 5: Wind on tide a mile offshore. A nasty sea, time to head home.

Force 8: No hope of getting out as huge waves break on shore. Stay at home.

Weather Service, the number of which will be in your local telephone directory. You can find out about sea conditions by telephoning your local coastguard, who will also be listed in the Post Office telephone book.

Shipping forecasts

Shipping forecasts for the 28 areas comprising the British Isles are broadcast on BBC Radio 2 (1500 metres) 200kHz at 0033, 0633, 1355 (1155 on Sundays) and at 1755. Gale warnings are also broadcast on this frequency as soon as possible after receipt and repeated, following the next news summary, on the hour.

Forecasts for inshore waters (up to 12 miles from the coast) are broadcast every evening on BBC Radio 4. The times on both medium wave and VHF frequencies vary around 2345 in different parts of the British Isles. Full details are given in the local editions of the *Radio Times*.

Special reports

Special forecasts for small boat users are broadcast on Radio 3 medium wave (464 metres/647kHz) on weekdays at 0655 and Saturday and Sunday at 0755.

Weather forecasts and gale warnings are also broadcast by Coast Radio Stations at times and on frequencies shown in the *Notice to Ship Wireless Stations* issued free by the GPO on application.

Information on local weather and sea conditions is given on the following BBC local stations (see panel at right).

Only a moderate north-westerly, but rocks are a dangerous place now.

RADIO STATION	VHF (MHz)	MED. WAVE (metres/kHz)
Bristol	95.5	194/1546
Blackburn	96.4	351/854
Brighton	95.3	202/1484
Carlisle	95.6	397/755
Cleveland	96.6	194/1546
Humberside	96.9	202/1484
Medway	96.7	290/1034
Merseyside	95.8	202/1484
Newcastle	95.4	206/1457
Solent	96.1	301/998

Small boats

(Left) This is the correct
way for two anglers to sit
in a boat while fishing.
All undue movement must be
avoided. Waterproof cushions
are necessary for long
periods on hard seats.
(Below) Always sit in a
small boat so that your
weight is balanced. If it
is at one end or the other
a wave may swamp it. The
rowing-boat is suitable
only for inshore fishing.

Ken Whitehead

A sea angler's first tentative trips should be
confined to sheltered waters and made under
the guidance of someone with experience.

If you are planning to buy a dinghy you
will want to know what size of boat is
adequate for sea trips and how many people
can be carried safely. There is a simple rule of
thumb to follow when making your choice.
For use in fine weather and inshore waters,
the minimum length of any boat should be
twice your height. The breadth, or beam,
should never be less than one third of the
length, while the internal depth should be
about an eighth of the length. Obviously a
man of 5ft weighing only a few stone is a
much safer load than one of, say, 6ft 6in, of
twice the weight. A small boy may be safe in
an eight-footer when a big man would be in
constant danger of upsetting the same craft.

Size of boat

How many people will a boat carry? Take the
largest person in the party and apply the
above rule. You will then need to increase the
length of boat required by roughly 1ft for
each additional passenger. More than three
anglers should not go out in a small boat.

Boat handling and seamanship are
acquired with practice and experience. But
there are basic principles which help the
novice. Of prime importance is 'trim', that is,

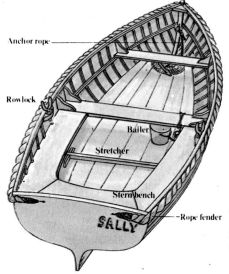

Anchor rope

Rowlock

Bailer

Stretcher

Stern bench

SALLY

Rope fender

Rod Sutterby

152

disposing the load in a boat so that she rides evenly in the water, neither down at the bow or stern, nor heeling to one side or the other. Never allow anyone to sit on the bow or sides of the boat. As far as possible keep weight out of the ends of the boat and she will lift easily on the waves. It is unwise to make any violent move aboard a boat; calm action and forethought are recommended. And keep the boat tidy. Stow your rods and tackle away until you are ready to begin fishing.

Launching

To launch from a beach—and no two beaches present the same problems since wind, tide and surf are constantly changing—you should copy the methods used by locals. On a simple shelving beach of shingle, with only small waves running, two men will bring a 12-14ft boat over the shingle on greased boards, stern first, until it is almost afloat, with waves reaching along almost half her length. One man will take his place in the middle of the boat with oars ready to push-row as soon as the boat floats, while the other waits for a 'smooth', pushes the boat far enough to be able to turn and head out to sea.

If the shore does not slope sufficiently to float the boat quickly, it will be necessary to launch bow first, with both men walking into the water pulling the boat until it floats. As the water deepens, one boards and rows from amidships to keep the boat heading into the waves while his helper steps aboard. The bow-first launch is again best when the beach is very steep so that the boat can be run down, with anglers already aboard, oars at the ready, by helpers who stay ashore.

If an outboard motor is to be used, the boat should be kept under way during the launch, using the oars, until the motor has been started and can take over, or the boat may turn and drift back into the surf should the motor prove obstinate. Outboard motors are now very popular, but the beginner should still learn to row proficiently at the outset, and see to it that his dinghy is provided with well-fitted rowlocks and oars of adequate size. He is then able to return safely if the engine fails.

Even if you do not intend to fish at anchor you must carry one and keep it ready for use. In the event of engine failure, broken oars or the like, the anchor is the only means of bringing the boat to a halt and countering wind and current. Be sure that the anchor is a good one with plenty of cable attached. The wind blowing offshore may leave a decep-

This small rowing-boat is suitable only for two of these anglers. Overcrowding is very dangerous and fishing impossible.

Bill Howes

(Left) Two anglers working well together while fishing from a small boat in Lough Carrane, Co. Kerry.
(Right) A fleet of small boats launching off the beach and a groyne at Folkestone for a day's sea angling.
(Below) Offshore winds can drag an anchored boat out to where the water is too deep for the anchor to be of any use.

Irish Tourist Board

tively smooth sea close inshore. Farther out it may blow stronger and can carry even an anchored boat out to where the sea roughens unless there is enough cable to give the anchor a good hold, and still more in reserve to pay out should it drag into deeper water. Three times the depth of water is the accepted guideline to cable length. The reserve should be led back over the prow to the middle of the boat and secured with an easily released hitch and neatly coiled. You can then handle the rope without moving forward. A 7lb anchor and 30 fathoms of $1\frac{1}{2}$in circumference rope will suffice for a dinghy in ordinary longshore conditions.

Always anchor from the bow, not the stern. The combined weight of an outboard motor and downward pull of the cable, were the anchor to snag, could quickly submerge the stern. It is good practice always to have your anchor rope clear and ready to slip should an emergency require you to move in a hurry. If, when doing so, you tie a buoy to the end of the rope before releasing it—an inflated plastic fender will serve—you will be able to return and recover the anchor when the danger has passed.

Essential equipment

A good compass must be taken, and once at anchor, or if visibility begins to deteriorate, take a bearing of the nearest safe landing place in case of sudden thick fog. In fine weather it will be possible to 'fix' your position, if not too far offshore, for you will be within sight of prominent buildings, hilltops and other natural landmarks.

An effective bailer with lanyard attached, is another essential. The lanyard may either

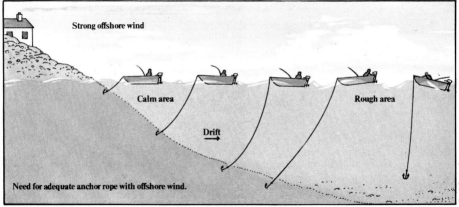

Strong offshore wind

Calm area

Rough area

Drift

Need for adequate anchor rope with offshore wind.

Rod Sutterby

be tied near the deepest part of the boat or a loop slipped over the wrist to stop it being lost overboard while bailing. Lanyards should also secure the rowlocks and even the outboard motor, which could disappear overboard if its clamp is loosened.

When at sea it is essential to keep a good lookout at all times. It is the unwritten law of the sea to go to the aid of anyone in distress. You can call for help yourself, but do not fire off *red* flares unless you are in real danger of drowning. If you have merely got into some difficulty which requires a tow home or other simple help—not the Search and Rescue Services—set off a white flare. All the information you need about safety equipment and so on is contained in 'The Seaway Code', obtainable free of charge from Coastguards, libraries, and seasport clubs.

Weather conditions

Pay attention to weather conditions both when you are afloat and before setting off. Even if the sea is calm, the sun shining and there is only a gentle breeze blowing, you should telephone the local weather station for an assurance of continuing good weather. The whole scene can change very rapidly. Consequently, the small boat sea angler should never venture far from a safe landing place or secure haven.

Acquaint yourself with tides and the strength and direction of tidal stream. It will greatly effect the time needed to travel out or home. A most useful item is the 'Pocket Tidal Stream Atlas', obtainable from agents for the sale of Admiralty charts. This shows graphically the strength and direction of tidal streams at any hour, before and after high water at Dover, in various areas of the coast. The time of high water at Dover is published in the daily press or is available in Tide Tables, which will also show the time of high water in your locality and tackle shops usually have these. Sometimes it is possible to leave after high water so that the current helps you on your way to the fishing ground, and fish for an hour or two until the tide turns so that the stream will help you home.

To bring the boat back onto gently shelving beaches the outboard motor can be kept running to bring the boat through the surf, but the bow must be kept as light as possible and the boat headed straight into the beach. The bow painter rope should be held ready by someone who remains back in the boat, ready to go forwards as soon as the boat is safely grounded but not a moment sooner. It is courting disaster to have someone forward, as his weight will depress the bow and swing the boat broadside onto the beach to be swamped by the waves.

Haul the boat up the beach out of the reach of the sea. If you are short of help on a long beach, carry all the gear up first to lighten the load. Where there are no greased boards or rollers, take out all removable parts including the bottom boards, turn the boat upside down and carry her!

Cruisers

When an angler wants to go sea fishing with greater comfort and safety than is possible in a dinghy, he will look to the many excellent inboard-engined launches which have been designed and built for the purpose of angling. Faced with a confusing number from which to choose, he will do well to make the acquaintance of sea anglers who own such boats in his locality. Thus he may learn of the advantages and shortcomings of at least some of the designs, and may find that one is a favourite for local conditions. Beware, though, of anyone who is trying to sell his boat to you. Even if he is completely honest, he may be unaware of incipient decay or a defect which only a qualified marine surveyor can detect.

Generally speaking, motorboats suitable for sea angling are those based on workboats and the semi-open types built for inshore professional fishermen. Those between 18ft and 30ft are the most popular. Boats of such size built specifically for 'cruising', with the maximum amount of sleeping accommodation, will not suit the keen angler; the cockpit will be too small, the area of her top-hamper exposed to the wind will make her unhandy, and space to work the anchor will be very restricted.

It is possible, of course, for the owner of such a craft to enjoy a spot of fishing while cruising, and he can sample the varied sport available while on his annual holiday, but his priorities will be quite different from the serious angler. On the other hand, boats of over 22ft can easily provide two berths in a forepeak and still have plenty of open space for half a dozen men to fish with rod and line.

Photo: Bill Howes

An armada heads out from Westport Quay towards the great complex of islands, where fishing is always possible.

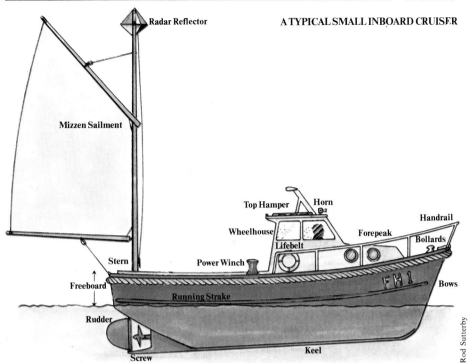

A TYPICAL SMALL INBOARD CRUISER

Radar Reflector

Mizzen Sailment

Top Hamper

Horn

Wheelhouse

Handrail

Forepeak

Lifebelt

Bollards

Stern

Power Winch

Freeboard

Bows

Running Strake

FH 1

Rudder

Screw

Keel

Rod Sutterby

The forepeak combined with steering cab will add greatly to the comfort by providing shelter from cool breezes which prevail in the best fishing season, and protection too, for navigational equipment. The area affected by wind will tend to make the boat lie awkwardly and sheer about when wind and tide are in opposition, so a mizzen sail will prove helpful in restoring the balance.

The heavy anchors needed by these bigger boats will tax the strength of the crew, especially in deeper waters. With an inboard engine, now almost universally diesel, a power winch eases this task.

For the novice owner

To gain experience before making a choice, and to get some idea of what is involved in working a boat, the novice owner will do well to book places in some of the boats which take out angling parties. Even though he may be an experienced angler, such trips will enable him to note what goes on, making a friend of the boat-man who is often an angler bitten by the sport to such an extent that he has taken up the job full-time. Skippers are often willing to let you help to work the boat. But do not make a nuisance of yourself.

Join a club, too, where boats are available or owned by fellow members many of whom will be able to give good advice. Some clubs and Local Authority evening classes will give instruction in seamanship and navigation.

Having acquired a powered boat our angler will have to get used to handling her before venturing out to sea, delighted with his new plaything—a marine Sunday motorist. For he will soon discover, perhaps before he succeeds in leaving the quay, that a boat does not react in any way like a motorcar.

He may swing the wheel, intending to steer away from the quayside, only to find that the bow does not move out, but that the stern swings in towards the wall, dragging along and preventing the bow from moving out. It is essential that he study the principles which govern the behaviour of a motorboat. The type of boat most commonly in use will have a long straight keel with a hull of moderate displacement, a single screw, and a rudder which will most probably be controlled by wheel steering. It is of first importance to discover the 'hand' of the screw as this has a very important effect on the movement of the vessel at low speeds. Because the blades are alternately in different depths of water the bottom blade is working in denser water and a greater degree of *pressure* is obtained there than in the upper blade thus pulling the stern *sideways* as well as pushing forward. This effect is greatest when the boat is

(Left) Angling cruisers need special features not always found on pleasure craft. First is plenty of room at the stern. Secondly, a powered winch for the anchor rope, worked from near the stern, is another important necessity, for skippers of charter-boats do not always have a crew. (Below) How to manoeuvre away from a quay.

stationary before it has had time to respond to the forward thrust of the screw. Its effect dies out as the boat gathers speed. When the screw is left-handed (it revolves anti-clockwise as viewed from astern) it will tend to thrust the stern to the left and vice versa if it is right-handed. With practice this allows the boat to be turned short round and manoeuvred in confined spaces when the natural turning circle of the boat at cruising speed is too great.

Turning with left-handed screw

To turn neatly round with a left-handed screw, let go the mooring and drift clear of it, engage for ahead and open the throttle to give a short burst, closing it again before the boat gathers way. You will find that the stern has begun to swing to the left and the bow to the right. Repeat this and you will increase the swing. You may let her begin to move ahead a little if it is necessary. When the boat moves ahead with the rudder in the central position, and the water flows evenly on both sides it has no effect, but when it is moved

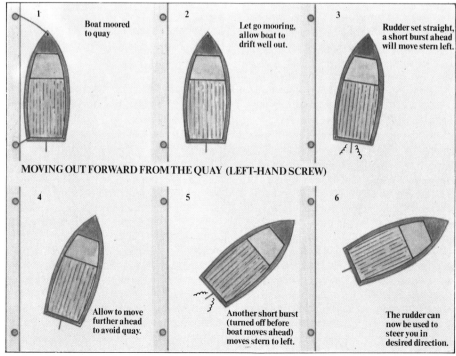

1 Boat moored to quay

2 Let go mooring, allow boat to drift well out.

3 Rudder set straight, a short burst ahead will move stern left.

MOVING OUT FORWARD FROM THE QUAY (LEFT-HAND SCREW)

4 Allow to move further ahead to avoid quay.

5 Another short burst (turned off before boat moves ahead) moves stern to left.

6 The rudder can now be used to steer you in desired direction.

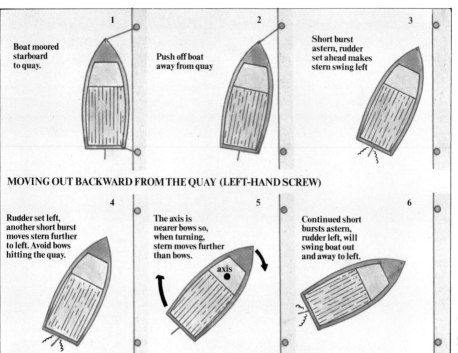

MOVING OUT BACKWARD FROM THE QUAY (LEFT-HAND SCREW)

1 Boat moored starboard to quay.

2 Push off boat away from quay

3 Short burst astern, rudder set ahead makes stern swing left

4 Rudder set left, another short burst moves stern further to left. Avoid bows hitting the quay.

5 The axis is nearer bows so, when turning, stern moves further than bows. axis

6 Continued short bursts astern, rudder left, will swing boat out and away to left.

Rod Sutterby

over to the right, pressure is built up on the forward side which will cause the stern to move to the left and further increase the movement of the bow to the right. Now with the boat swinging nicely but beginning to move ahead it may be necessary to check the forward movement. With throttle closed as the boat slows, engage the gear astern and put the rudder to left. Open the throttle again and the thrust from the screw (pushing water forward onto the back of the rudder) will help you keep the stern swinging to the left, as will the force of the water flowing past the rudder as the boat moves astern. The amount of movement, both forward and astern, must be carefully restricted so as to allow the swinging movement to be the greatest. This routine is best tried out where there is plenty of room and little wind.

Applying the technique

Having mastered the technique it can then be applied to get neatly away from alongside a quay. If the boat is lying right side to it, a touch ahead (with the left-hand propellor),

(Above) Backing away from a quay by means of a left-handed screw. First push the boat off; then a short burst, with the rudder straight to swing the stern out. When in motion, turn the rudder left. Short bursts of the engine will pull the craft away.
(Right) The busy air of charter boats soon to be on their way to the marks.

will begin to swing the stern away. When her stern is far enough out to keep the bow from scraping along the quay, go astern with the rudder to the left. If the boat has a right-handed screw the very opposite applies and the boat would need to be lying with its left side to the quay to obtain this effect and the rudder put to the right.

It will help the initial outward swing of the stern when leaving the quay if the bow is held by keeping fast the 'bow spring', while the first touch ahead is given to stop the forward movement, allowing the ahead time to be prolonged thus getting the maximum effect from the sideways thrust of the screw. Only when the stern is well out should the rope be freed and the screw reversed.

This method of getting away from the quay is particularly useful when the wind is blowing onto the quay, for it is one of the peculiarities of boat behaviour that when she is going astern the *rudder* has less affect than when going *ahead* but her *screw* has *more*. It will pull her astern to windward better than it can push her bow out against the wind. If caught between quays with the wind astern and an obstruction ahead and your boat refuses to turn short enough to get her round into the wind, put her in reverse. Then, as she begins to move astern, the pivot point will move right aft and the bow blow away from the wind, letting the screw take the boat stern-first to windward out of trouble.

Effect of wind and current

Angling launches and workboats are often fitted with a large fender around the bows to facilitate this manoeuvre by protecting the stem from damage should it bear on the quay. The wind and current, if any, will affect manoeuvring when coming alongside and you will have to judge which will have the greater effect. When approaching with the wind from ahead its effect varies with the height of the bows and depth of the forefoot. The slower the boat, the more the wind will catch the bow and blow it off course, and with too great an angle of approach will blow the bows onto the quay. The gear must be put into neutral at a point where the boat will soon stop, lying at an angle of about 20° with her bow just off the quay. The rudder should then be put over to force her stern towards the quay and the screw put slow ahead when she will drop nicely alongside as the gear is again put to neutral. *Do not* do this with a burst or you will induce the sideways action of the propellor which may overcome the force of the rudder.

Berthing in following wind

If the wind is from *astern* as you approach your berth, take plenty of room; carry on well past the spot, turn, then approach head-to-wind. If the current is stronger than the effect of the wind, approach head-to-current

but take care to watch the way the wind is affecting your approach. The bow rope should be passed ashore and secured first, the stern rope following as soon after as possible.

Do not let your crew throw ropes until you are quite sure you are going to complete the manoeuvre successfully, for it is better to go off and approach again if you have muffed it. A rope secured ashore too soon will inhibit this, while if it misses, it may get around the screw, when you will be really in trouble.

It is not possible to include even the fraction of all you should learn in this short article, but finally you would be well advised to register your boat with H.M. Coastguard Yacht & Boat Safety Scheme. All you need to do is fill in a simple post-paid card obtainable from the Safety Scheme 'Issuing Authority' at clubs, harbour offices, marinas or Coastguard Stations, and send it back to the Coastguard. It will be retained at the Coastguard Rescue Headquarters for your area.

Bill Howes